HOW IN THE WORLD DO STUDENTS READ?

IEA STUDY OF READING LITERACY

THE IEA STUDY OF READING LITERACY

THE STUDY IN BRIEF

Countries

In 1990-1991 thirty-two school systems were involved in the IEA Reading Literacy Study. Participating in the study were:

Belgium (French)	Germany (West)	Netherlands	Spain
Botswana	Greece	New Zealand	Sweden
Canada (BC)	Hong Kong	Nigeria	Switzerland
Cyprus	Hungary	Norway	Thailand
Denmark	Iceland	Philippines	Trinidad & Tobago
Finland	Indonesia	Portugal	United States
France	Ireland	Singapore	Venezuela
Germany (East)	Italy	Slovenia	Zimbabwe

Data was collected from a very large number of schools, teachers and students. The size of the study can be seen from the total numbers involved.

1990-1991	Schools	Teachers	Students
Population A	4,353	4,992	93,039
Population B	4,720	5,526	117,020
Total	9,073	10,518	210,059

Target Populations

Population A: All students attending school on a full-time basis at the grade level in which most students aged 9:00-9:11 years were enrolled during the first week of the eighth month of the school year.

Population B: All students attending school on a full-time basis at the grade level in which most students aged 14:00-14:11 years were enrolled during the first week of the eighth month of the school year.

Testing Program

All students took reading tests for two sessions totaling 75 minutes at the Population A level and two sessions totaling 85 minutes at the Population B level.

Questionnaires

All students responded to a background questionnaire about their reading at home and at school. Teachers and school principals responded to questionnaires about themselves, their teaching and the school organization. Each National Center completed a National Case Study Questionnaire.

WARWICK B. ELLEY

How in the world do students read?

IEA STUDY OF READING LITERACY

**The International Association
for the Evaluation of Educational Achievement**

July 1992

Cover by Weidmüller Design

Printed for IEA in Germany by
GRINDELDRUCK GMBH, Hamburg

ArtOnLine, Hamburg

Second printing

ISBN: 92-9121-002-3

PREFACE

In the late 1950s a group of leading educational research workers met in England and at the Unesco Institute of Education in Hamburg to discuss common problems in the conduct of educational research. From their deliberations they recognized the need for a comparative research program that was empirically oriented and that investigated problems which were common to many national systems of education. They saw the world of education as a natural laboratory in which different countries were experimenting with different strategies of teaching and learning. By examining the naturally occurring differences between countries in both the conditions of learning and educational outcomes, they thought it might be possible to identify the significant factors that influenced educational achievement. The program of research would be both comparative and cooperative. Decisions were to be made through scholarly debate and not political pressure. Members of the organization would be research centers and scholars with the competence to undertake survey research. For over 30 years the organization that developed from these early discussions has undertaken a continuing program of research. This organization, formally called the International Association for the Evaluation of Educational Achievement, is now commonly referred to as IEA.

In 1988, the IEA General Assembly, composed of the research institutes participating in IEA projects, decided to undertake a study of Reading Literacy. A Steering Committee of six members was formed and a technical advisory group appointed. (See Appendix A for a list of study personnel.) The chairperson of the Steering Committee was Professor Warwick B. Elley from New Zealand. He is the author of this first booklet of a series and presents the preliminary results of the study. An International Coordinating Center (ICC) was established at the Faculty of Education at the University of Hamburg, Germany, under the direction of Professor T. Neville Postlethwaite. Research institutes from thirty-two systems of education participated in the study. Each of them appointed a National Research Coordinator (NRC) to be responsible for the day-to-day running of the study in their own countries. All conceptual and operational decisions were made cooperatively by the Steering Committee and NRCs.

The study held its first NRC meeting in November 1988. The construction and pilot testing of instruments was conducted in the period November 1988 to July 1990. The main testing took place in the period October 1990 to April 1991 depending on the school year in each country.

The national costs of conducting the study were borne by the research institutes acting as the National Centers in each country. The international costs, amounting to US $615,000 from November 1988 to May 1992, came from the participating countries themselves, the MacArthur Foundation, the Mellon

Foundation, the National Center for Educational Statistics through the National Academy of Sciences, the European Community, the Maxwell Family Foundation and Unesco.

The study could not have been conducted without a great deal of goodwill, support, and cooperation from the National Centers involved in the study. The members of the Steering Committee and the Technical Advisers worked without financial recompense of any kind. NRC meetings were hosted by some of the National Centers.

IEA thanks all of those involved for their contributions to this major international investigation. In particular, IEA thanks Professor Warwick B. Elley, the author of this first booklet to emerge from the IEA Reading Literacy Study. His commitment and unstinting work for the study have been enormous.

T. Plomp
Chairman of IEA

About the Author

Warwick B. Elley is Professor of Education at the University of Canterbury in New Zealand. He has taught in both primary and secondary schools. He has a Ph.D. in Education Measurement from the University of Alberta (Canada) and gained much practical experience in test construction when he was Assistant Director of the New Zealand Council for Educational Research (NZCER) in the 1970s.

His research work has involved the conduct of national assessments of achievement (including reading) in New Zealand, Indonesia, Singapore, and several Pacific Islands. Some of these countries were involved in the Reading Literacy Study.

His 25 year association with the International Reading Association has given him insight into the world of literacy. He has won several awards for his research on the promotion and assessment of children's literacy.

He is the author of a number of books and many research reports on reading and assessment. As chairperson of the IEA Reading Literacy Study he was able to visit nineteen of the participating countries in order to visit schools and talk to local educators.

It is clear that Warwick B. Elley, with his practical knowledge, research experience, and international perspectives, is an eminent person in the area of Reading Literacy. IEA is pleased that he agreed to be the Chairperson of the Steering Committee and the author of this first booklet.

Tjeerd Plomp
Chairman of IEA

CONTENTS

IEA STUDY OF READING LITERACY
EXECUTIVE SUMMARY

This booklet focuses on the reading literacy test scores of students in the grade levels where most 9- and 14-year-olds were to be found in 32 systems of education. It describes the achievement levels of carefully selected probability samples of students in three domains of reading literacy and makes some preliminary interpretations of these results.

The comparisons made in the test scores require the reader to assume that the tests were equally fair for all countries, that the tests were properly translated and administered, and that the student samples were comparable in age, in test motivation, and in their approach to test-taking. Much effort was taken to ensure and to check on these possible influences. Where differences were still found to exist – for instance, in mean ages – comments have been made in the text and adjustments to the scores have been attempted.

The following findings have emerged from the initial analyses of this survey of achievement.

1. *National achievement levels.*
   The students of FINLAND showed the highest reading literacy levels at both 9 and 14 years of age in almost all domains. Students in the UNITED STATES also produced relatively high scores at the nine-year-old level, and in SWEDEN, FRANCE, and NEW ZEALAND at the fourteen-year-old level.

2. *Domain profiles.*
   The levels of reading literacy achieved in each country are highly correlated across all three domains, and across both age groups. However, fourteen-year-old students in CYPRUS and GREECE showed greater strength in the Narrative domain, while students in HONG KONG, SWITZERLAND, GERMANY and DENMARK performed better in Documents at both age levels.

3. *Economic and social context.*
   For most countries, the levels of reading literacy are closely related to their national indices of economic development, health, and adult literacy. Nevertheless, HONG KONG attained high levels of achievement at both age levels with only average status on these developmental indices. Nine-year-olds in FINLAND and ITALY, and fourteen-year-olds in HUNGARY, PORTUGAL and SINGAPORE also achieved well above the scores expected on the basis of developmental indices.

4. *Home language.*
   The students of SINGAPORE achieved high levels of literacy in spite of the fact that they were instructed in a non-native language from the beginning of their schooling. This finding is unexpected and potentially important.

5. *Age of beginning instruction.*
   Formal instruction did not begin until age seven in four of the ten highest-scoring countries at each level. Apparently a late start is not a serious handicap in reading instruction, when judged at age nine. However, when achievement scores were adjusted for economic and social circumstances across all countries, an earlier start was generally found to be an advantage.
6. *Differences between high- and low-scoring countries.*
   Factors which consistently differentiated high-scoring and low-scoring countries were large school libraries, large classroom libraries, regular book borrowing, frequent silent reading in class, frequent story reading aloud by teachers, and more scheduled hours spent teaching the language. Several countries with low scores reported very little experience with formal tests, but above a threshold level, this factor was not found to differentiate high- and low-achieving countries. At the 14-year-old level, additional factors which helped differentiate high-scoring countries from low-scoring countries were more general homework, more literacy resources in the school, more individual tuition, fewer non-native speaking teachers, a shorter school year, and more female teachers.
7. *Less important differentiating factors.*
   At the nine-year-old level, no perceptible advantage was found in reading literacy levels of countries which had high enrollment ratios in preschool, or generally smaller classes, or large numbers of multi-grade classes, or longer school years, or policies of keeping the teachers with the same class through successive grades. While many of these policies were found regularly in high-scoring countries, the data suggest that their importance may well be only a function of relative affluence and community factors outside the school.
8. *Gender differences.*
   Girls achieved at higher levels than boys in all countries in Population A, and in most countries in Population B. The mean difference, favoring girls, dropped from 12 points to 7 points at age fourteen. Girls showed the largest advantage in the Narrative domain, and the smallest in Documents. In countries which begin formal instruction at age five, boys showed lower scores, relative to girls.
9. *Language differences.*
   Children whose home language is different from that of the school show lower literacy levels in all countries at both age levels. The differences between these children and speakers of the language of instruction are greatest in NEW ZEALAND in both populations.
10. *Urban-rural differences.*
    Urban children achieve at higher levels than rural children in most education systems. However, in a few highly developed countries, rural students show literacy levels which are as good as, or better than their city age mates.

11. *Importance of books.*

    The availability of books is a key factor in reading literacy. The highest scoring countries typically provide their students with greater access to books in the home, in nearby community libraries and book stores, and in the school.

12. *Links with television.*

    Television viewing occupies much of students' out-of-school discretionary time. In a few countries large numbers of children watch TV for more than five hours per day. Those who watch TV often tend to score at lower levels than those who watch less, as a general rule. However, in a small number of countries, children who watch for three to four hours daily have the highest reading scores. In these countries imported films with subtitles in the local language are often shown.

13. *Self-ratings.*

    Within all countries, good readers perceive themselves to be above average in reading ability on the whole, but the accuracy of their judgments varies considerably across countries. Students of FINLAND, HONG KONG, SINGAPORE, and HUNGARY are relatively modest about their reading; students of GREECE, CYPRUS, the UNITED STATES and CANADA (BC) are relatively confident.

14. *Becoming a good reader.*

    When asked how they could become good readers, students in most countries emphasized such factors as *Liking it, Having lots of time to read,* and *Concentrating well.* Younger students in many countries also stressed *Knowing how to sound out words*, especially in SPAIN and VENEZUELA, but not in NORWAY, NEW ZEALAND and HONG KONG. The best readers in the high-scoring countries emphasized *Having many good books around, Learning many new words* and *Doing many written exercises.* By contrast, the best readers in low-scoring countries stressed *Sounding out the words, Regular drill on the hard things*, and *Doing much reading for homework.* These national differences are believed to reflect variations in teaching emphases.

15. *Voluntary reading.*

    The amount of voluntary out-of-school book reading that students report is positively related to their achievement levels. This relationship is clearer at the 9-year-old level, and in the developing countries at age fourteen. However, the findings reveal an optimum level of voluntary book and magazine reading in Population B beyond which additional reading appears not to enhance achievement as judged by these tests.

CHAPTER ONE

WHAT IS THE STUDY ABOUT?

The Challenge

To acquire the ability to read is a fundamental human right and a basic requirement for individual and national development in the 1990s. Yet for nearly one fifth of the earth's population, the printed word has nothing to say. The Unesco publication, *World Education Report 1991,* states that more than 950 million adults are unable to read and write (Unesco 1991, p. 22). Moreover, educators around the world hold widely differing views about how best to teach students to read.

In many countries phonics teaching is paramount; in a few, phonics is a dirty word. In some systems primary school begins at age five; in others, it is delayed until age seven. In many nations students work systematically through commercially produced sets of graded readers; in others students are believed to learn best through a rich and varied diet of children's literature. Teachers in some countries insist on regular workbook exercises; elsewhere they require only that children enjoy and talk about what they read. Some argue strongly for small group activities; others believe children should be taught as a whole class.

There are many other differences in policies between nations – from the number of days spent in school to the training of teachers, the size of classes, the frequency of testing, and the extent of homework, to name but a few. Many of these differences are debated within countries; others are nationwide traditions and taken for granted by most educators and parents.

An international study of these diverse policies is well justified in itself. If such a study also attempts to relate them to carefully devised indicators of the levels of achievement reached in reading literacy by students in each country, it may well be able to throw important light on which, if any of these policies have important consequences for students' progress in reading. The researchers involved in the study accepted this challenge – to assess differences in the reading achievement levels and voluntary reading activities of 9- and 14-year-old students in each of 32 systems of education, and to link these differences to variations in policies and practices across countries. It proved an awesome challenge, and many critics of literacy assessment procedures across languages and cultures questioned its feasibility. However, the challenge was accepted, as the likely benefits appeared to outweigh the costs, and the results of pilot tests conducted in many of the countries greatly increased the researchers' optimism about the viability of the project.

This booklet reports the initial results of this enormous international research exercise, the largest of its kind. The report describes and attempts to interpret the average achievement levels in reading literacy of some 210,000 children in 32 educational systems on every continent of the earth. For each country the report breaks down these outcome measures by gender, home background, native language, book resources, and other sub-groups of interest. More detailed analyses are reported in a number of booklets and in a full international report. A separate technical report presents more technical details.

The Study

How was the study conducted?

The International Association for the Evaluation of Educational Achievement (IEA), which conducted the study, is a network of national educational research organizations in some 50 countries. It was created in order to carry out comparative surveys of schooling in its member countries. The IEA General Assembly approved the Reading Literacy Study in 1986 and planning was undertaken by an International Steering Committee (appointed by the IEA General Assembly) with the aid of representatives from each of 35 participating countries, starting in Washington, DC, in late 1988. An International Coordinating Center was established in Hamburg, Germany (see Appendix A for persons involved in the study).

The Steering Committee, consisting of researchers from six countries, proposed the major aims and guidelines. These were modified and extended at several international meetings by representatives, called National Research Coordinators (NRCs), from each participating institution. Items for the tests and questionnaires were generated, translated and pilot tested by these NRCs in 1989-1990. After analysis of the pilot data by the research staff at the International Coordinating Center in Hamburg, the final tests were selected by the Steering Committee and NRCs in July 1990.

The formal survey was conducted on scientifically selected national samples of 9- and 14-year-olds, typically 1,500 to 3,000 pupils per country, and their teachers in 1990-1991. The tests and questionnaires were administered under standardized conditions to the national samples in the eighth month of the school year of 1990-1991. Southern hemisphere countries administered the tests six months earlier to coincide with their school year.

Where necessary, tests were translated into the local language under the supervision of NRCs and according to guidelines provided by the Steering Committee. Two parallel translations of the tests were requested and back translations were asked for on sample passages and items as a check for accuracy. Further checks were conducted by studying the patterns of item analysis results across countries. Layout, illustrations, instructions, and time limits were standardized, but minor cultural adaptations were permitted to allow for more suitable place names, people's names, local currencies and measurement units.

What were the major aims of the study?

As in earlier IEA studies, the Steering Committee gave priority to the task of surveying achievement levels in comparable samples of students in each country. The first aim then, accepted by all, was to determine the average levels of reading literacy of representative samples of all students in the grades where most 9- and 14-year-olds were to be found. These two groups were called Population A and Population B respectively.

This aim is the focus of this report. Why choose the grade levels of 9- and 14-year-olds? An earlier IEA study of reading achievement in 15 countries (Thorndike 1973) had chosen 10-year-olds as the first population to be surveyed. However, the author suggested in hindsight, that a younger age might have been more fruitful. It might well allow the identification of important factors associated with learning to read. The age of 14 years was set as the most suitable for the survey of older students because it was found to be the final year of compulsory schooling in many countries. Thus it represented the level of achievement in literacy likely to be attained by school leavers in these countries. Such levels represent the quality of reading to be expected in the next generation of citizens.

Other aims adopted by NRCs, some of which are reported on in later publications, include the following:

- To describe the voluntary reading activities of 9- and 14-year-olds;
- To identify differences in policies and instructional practices in reading, and to study the ways in which they relate to students' achievement and voluntary reading;
- To produce valid international tests and questionnaires which could be used to investigate reading literacy development in other countries;
- To provide national baseline data suitable for monitoring changes in reading literacy levels and patterns over time.

What is reading literacy?

For the purposes of the study, reading literacy was defined as:

> . . .*the ability to understand and use those written language forms required by society and/or valued by the individual.*

Such a definition was found to be general enough to accommodate the diversity of traditions and languages represented in the participating countries, but specific enough to provide some guidance for test construction. Writing ability was deliberately excluded from the definition, and only a minimal amount of writing was required of students throughout the testing process. The emphasis on language forms required by society reflects the concept of functional literacy and coping with reading tasks frequently encountered in an organized society – reading notices, newspapers, maps, graphs and government circulars. However, a broader definition was required to meet the needs of many

National Committees who argued for the inclusion of higher-level thinking and the interpretation of narrative prose and magazine articles. Hence the additional notion of materials *valued by the individual*. While the majority of NRCs favored an emphasis on both *understanding* and *use*, the constraints of mass testing, standardized conditions, traditional policies, and limited school time in many nations, made it imperative that the major stress be placed on *understanding*. Nevertheless, it was found possible to measure students' ability to follow directions in a few tasks.

The major domains or types of reading literacy materials to be included in the final tests of both age levels were as follows:

1. *Narrative prose:* Continuous texts in which the writer's aim is to tell a story – whether fact or fiction. They normally follow a linear time sequence and are usually intended to entertain or involve the reader emotionally. The selected extracts ranged from short fables to lengthy stories of more than 1,000 words.

2. *Expository prose:* Continuous texts designed to describe, explain, or otherwise convey factual information or opinion to the reader. The tests contained, for example, brief family letters and descriptions of animals as well as lengthy treatises on smoking and lasers.

3. *Documents:* Structured information displays presented in the form of charts, tables, maps, graphs, lists or sets of instructions. These materials were organized in such a way that students had to search, locate and process selected facts rather than read every word of continuous text. In some cases, students were required to follow detailed instructions in responding to such documents.

Other forms of classifying reading tasks were investigated and are used when appropriate in other publications of this series.

The Tests

What form did the tests take?

In order to demonstrate their levels of reading literacy, students had to read a balanced sample of each of the three types of materials, and answer questions to show how well they could understand and/or use them. The expository and document materials were drawn from typical *home, school, society* or *work* contexts, with a somewhat greater emphasis on the school. From the outset, it was agreed that test scores would be reported separately for each of the three domains – Narrative, Expository and Documents.

Another type of task, a Word Recognition Test, was added for the 9-year-old students. This task required students to match simple, individual words with a corresponding picture (selected out of four), and was administered under speeded conditions. It provided weaker students with a task they could manage, and was designed to show whether weaknesses observed in reading comprehension in a group of students could be attributed to their inability to decode quickly words of high familiarity.

One way to produce a clear operational definition of the nature of reading literacy, as interpreted in this study, is to present a two-way blueprint of the tests classified by domain (Table 1.1).

Table 1.1. Two-way blueprint of tests by domain.

Domains	Population A (9-year-olds)		Population B (14-year-olds)	
	No. of passages	No. of items	No. of passages	No. of items
Word Recognition	--	40*	--	--
Narrative	4	22	5	29
Expository	5	21	5	26
Documents	6	23	9	34
Total	15	66	19	89

*The Word Recognition items were not included in the analysis of the main set of test items.

What kinds of test items were used?

Students in most countries were familiar with the multiple-choice format and this type was preferred by most NRCs. Such items were considered to be both objective and versatile and to be quickly scored, an important consideration in large surveys. However, a number of NRCs made a case for including more open-ended items on the grounds that they were more life-like and could assess important higher level outcomes not measured by objective tests. On the other hand, the practical difficulties and cost of scoring the responses counted against the use of such items. In order to throw more light on this issue, two members of the Steering Committee conducted a study of multiple-choice versus open-ended items on the same reading passages drawn from the pilot tests for 9-year-olds. The results of this study (Elley and Mangubhai 1992) confirmed the findings of other such studies in reading, namely, that in reading surveys both types of items measure essentially the same abilities, and that multiple-choice items do so in less time, with less cost and are more popular with students. While there are clear reasons for using more open-ended questions in diagnostic testing and other classroom assessment, the value of including many such items in an international survey of reading literacy had not been empirically demonstrated before this study was conducted. In the final tests, however, there were four completion-type items (one- or two-word answers) and two paragraph-length answers selected for inclusion in the 9-year-olds' test, and twenty completion-type and two paragraph-length answers in the 14-year-olds' test. The paragraph-length answers were scored locally and were not included in the international data reported here. Appendix B reports further information on the international validity of the Reading Literacy tests.

How were the tests scored?

To obtain raw scores, all correct answers were totaled for each student in each domain. The Rasch procedure was used to produce scales for each domain. Each scale was given a mean of 500 and a standard deviation of 100. The meaning of these scores is explained when the results are presented in Chapters 3 and 4. The rationale for the scoring procedure is given in Appendix C.

What other information was collected?

At meetings of the NRCs, the following questionnaires were designed to obtain information from each system about factors related to reading.
1. Student Questionnaires on the students' home and school circumstances;
2. Teacher Questionnaires on each teacher's background, instructional practices and beliefs;
3. School Questionnaires on the school circumstances and policies as viewed by the principal;
4. National Case Study Questionnaires completed by NRCs on national policy, enrollment patterns and economic conditions.

Who was tested?

In each country, Population A consisted of the students in the grade level containing the most 9-year-olds, and Population B consisted of the students in the grade level containing the most 14-year-olds (see Appendix D for details).

To obtain comparable samples of students, multi-stage sampling was used in each country and schools or classes were typically drawn with a probability proportional to the size of the school or class. Where schools were drawn, an intact class was selected at random within each school, but in Population B some NRCs selected students at random from all classes in the grade level in the school.

To overcome fluctuations in the execution of the sampling, weighting was used to adjust for any variations in the probability of selecting students. These sampling weights were used in all data analyses.

In three of the smaller countries, all students in the relevant grade level were tested. Further details on sampling are given in Appendix D. It should be noted that most countries achieved over 90 percent response rates. Only ITALY, PORTUGAL, the UNITED STATES and VENEZUELA had between 80 and 90 percent in the Population A sample. In NIGERIA, THAILAND and ZIMBABWE the number of schools or classes in the Population B sample was actually less than 80 percent of the classes in the planned sample.

CHAPTER TWO

A WORD ON INTERNATIONAL COMPARISONS

What Cautions Should Be Observed?

In comparing various countries – or anything else, for that matter – one should examine the degree to which the bases for the comparisons are fair and valid. Besides differing in language and culture, countries differ substantially in wealth, development, and the resources available to education. Is it fair and valid to compare the performance of countries that vary in so many different ways? Is it possible to adjust the performance levels of countries to make comparisons fair and valid? There are no clear answers to these questions. The fairness and validity of any comparison are matters of degree, and the adequacy of any comparison will depend on the use to which it is put and the alternatives available for decision-making. Are there better bases for making judgments?

The design and implementation of this study of reading literacy has attempted to make international comparisons as fair and valid as possible, although still imperfect. There exist at least three threats to fair and valid comparisons: the student population, the reading tests, and the translation process. More detailed discussion of these factors is presented in the Technical Report.

The student populations

An obvious problem in international comparisons is that different nations may be represented by substantially different populations as, for example, if the elite students of one nation are compared with the general population of another. To avoid this pitfall, the researchers defined the student populations at grade levels at which almost all students were in school. In practice, a few countries varied from this definition because sampling non-government schools could not be done or because the testing of language minorities was impractical. These exceptions are noted in the appropriate places. In each country, probability samples of the *defined* populations were selected under the supervision of an international sampling coordinator to ensure fair representations from the defined population, and almost all nations met the stringent sampling requirements. However, varying educational policies on age of entry to school and retention versus age promotion resulted in some small but noticeable differences in the ages and grades of the student populations. Thus, countries did vary in the proportions of 9-year-olds and 14-year-olds in the grades they selected. The effects of these differences are discussed in Appendix E.

The tests of reading literacy

Comparisons would clearly be unfair if the measuring instrument represented the curricular emphasis of only one or a few different countries. To avoid this problem, all countries were invited to submit questions for inclusion in the international test, and most of them did. The test, therefore, is representative of the reading curriculum and achievement criteria in many countries, and in a sense is a consensus of what students in different countries are expected to be able to do. The pools of items generated by the NRCs were trialled and pretested by an extensive series of pilot tests that were designed to ensure that the items operated in a similar fashion in the countries participating in the study. The final selection of items was agreed upon by the NRCs and their National Committees. However, this care in constructing an international test cannot remove bias that might emerge due to differences in familiarity with testing in general, or with multiple-choice items in particular. (See Appendix B for more details.)

The translation process

Any translation process entails the possibility that the meaning is lost in translation, and an international test is no exception. To guard against this type of bias, test items were translated independently from the source language by native speakers according to common guidelines, then compared and revised. Every effort was made to ensure that the original sense of the text and items was maintained. Moreover, the items were examined after the pilot test and again after the final test to ensure that they behaved similarly in different countries. (See Appendix B for more details on the comparability of tests.)

   Despite the extensive effort to make international comparisons as fair and valid as possible, there is a point beyond which the technical aspects of the study cannot reach. In general this report presents the simple data summaries and leaves the reader to judge the adequacy of the comparisons. Throughout the report, threats to validity and fairness will be noted. It is argued, frankly, that these comparisons – either adjusted or not adjusted – are useful for many purposes and are certainly better than alternative comparisons made without carefully controlled empirical data. In the end, however, each reader must decide for him or herself whether a comparison is adequate for a particular purpose.

How Do Countries Vary in their Economic
and Cultural Contexts of Literacy Education?

Some nations are able to give their children a head start in any comparison of achievement levels in reading literacy. Where students typically come from literate, economically secure homes and attend well-resourced schools with well-qualified teachers one would expect higher achievement levels. By contrast, there are some countries where the level of economic and social development is low and literacy traditions are still limited. Inevitably, there will be fewer schools in such places that are well-endowed with libraries, textbooks and well-trained teachers.

Table 2.1. Selected national indicators of development in 32 participating countries and the Composite Development Index (CDI).

Country	(1) GNP per capita ($US)	(2) Public exp. per student on educ. ($US)	(3) Life expect-ancy	(4) % Low birth weight	(5) News-papers per 1000 pop	(6) % Adult literacy	Com-posite devel. index	CDI rank
Belgium/Fr	14,490	2,772	75	5	219	99	3.41	13
Botswana	1,010	292	67	8	16	71	1.63	29
Canada/BC	16,960	4,096	77	6	254	99	3.66	7
Cyprus	5,200	902	75	---	125	---	2.74	21.5
Denmark	18,450	3,390	75	6	359	99	3.64	10
Finland	18,590	2,989	75	4	551	99	3.89	5
France	16,090	2,912	76	5	193	99	3.48	11
Germany/E	11,300	1,697	73	6	585	99	3.44	12
Germany/W	18,480	3,021	75	5	347	99	3.65	8.5
Greece	4,800	462	77	6	102	93	2.74	21.5
Hong Kong	9,220	843	77	---	239	88	2.85	18
Hungary	2,460	768	70	10	273	98	2.51	24
Iceland	16,596	---	77	3	562	99	3.98	4
Indonesia	440	54	61	14	21	74	1.06	31
Ireland	7,750	1,349	74	4	175	99	3.09	16
Italy	13,330	1,894	77	7	105	97	3.13	15
Netherlands	14,520	2,910	77	4	314	99	3.65	8.5
New Zealand	10,000	1,261	75	5	327	99	3.25	14
Nigeria	290	294	51	20	22	43	0.51	32
Norway	19,990	4,462	77	4	551	99	4.15	3
Philippines	630	29	64	18	56	86	1.28	30
Portugal	3,650	459	74	8	41	85	2.31	25
Singapore	9,070	1,252	74	7	289	86	2.78	20
Slovenia	6,500	374	73	5	151	99	2.97	17
Spain	7,740	630	77	---	75	95	2.79	19
Sweden	19,300	5,317	77	4	526	99	4.20	2
Switzerland	27,500	5,274	77	5	504	99	4.29	1
Thailand	1,000	139	65	12	48	91	1.75	27
Trinidad/Tobago	3,350	1,600	71	---	139	96	2.64	23
United States	19,840	4,220	76	7	259	99	3.67	6
Venezuela	3,250	756	70	9	164	87	2.23	26
Zimbabwe	650	141	63	15	24	83	1.65	28
Mean	10,076	1,824	72.53	7.64	236.4	91.9	2.91	
SD	7,561	1,627	6.04	4.37	182.5	11.7	0.96	

* Estimated from Unesco reports; typically four years of schooling.

Note: The six national indicators were combined with equal weight to produce the Composite Development Index (CDI) for each country.

In order to provide a framework within which to judge more fairly the results of this survey, the average scores for each participating country are presented alongside a measure of certain relevant indicators of national development. Table 2.1 lists a set of six indicators chosen to highlight national differences in three kinds of resources – *economic*, *health* and *literacy* – plus a Composite Development Index (CDI) formed by aggregating all six indicators. These three basic dimensions of national development were chosen because they are believed to provide indirect support to the promotion of literacy levels in schools, over and above the quality of their teaching programs. They are readily available indicators, reasonably accurate, generally stable over time and relevant for interpreting the progress of literacy in each country.

Thus, nations with a high *GNP* can afford to pay more for quality teachers, for teacher training, for advisory services, and for better resources in schools. The actual *expenditure on education per student* is another indicator of both national wealth and the value placed on education by the community. Indices such as *life expectancy* and the *percentage of low birth-weight infants* are indirect measures of general physical health. The inclusion of health measures is based on the assumption that students' schooling, if it is to be successful, will not be handicapped by malnutrition, inadequate health services, and frequent absences from school, on the part of students or teachers. The *number of newspapers* in circulation per 1000 population and the reported *percentage of adult literacy* are both indirect measures of the value placed on literacy by the general population. Countries with low status on the CDI are systematically disadvantaged on these criteria, and thus are potentially less able to achieve high levels of literacy on the tests used in this survey.

The decision to combine these indicators into a single index of development was assisted by recent precedents and by the very high correlation observed among them in this survey (see Appendix F). The three underlying dimensions are similar to those reported in the recent Human Development Index (HDI) produced by a UNDP team (1991). This index was based on GDP, Life Expectancy and Adult Literacy Level. The addition of three more indices, each of which was highly correlated with one of the HDI dimensions, was believed to strengthen the statistical base of the CDI, and to reduce the effects of minor anomalies due to differences in methods of reporting the HDI indicators. The correlation between the CDI used in the survey and the HDI for 32 systems was 0.89. The development of the CDI makes possible a fairer interpretation of the differences between nations in their reading literacy standards, as reported in this booklet.

CHAPTER THREE

HOW WELL DO NINE-YEAR-OLDS READ AROUND THE WORLD?

General Comments

What scores are used for reporting?

This chapter presents the achievement scores for Population A students in the 27 countries which participated at this age level. Before these scores are given, however, it is appropriate to explain briefly what they mean.

In Table 1.1 it was seen that the Population A Narrative domain had 22 items. The Rasch scaling method was used to create an international scale which has a mean of 500 and a standard deviation of 100. All Narrative scores for the 9-year-old samples are reported on this scale. The same procedure was used for reporting student scores in each domain and at each age level. Thus, there are three separate domain scales for each age level used for reporting in this booklet. There is no particular significance in a scale which centers on 500 points. Like temperature scales which can be reported in Fahrenheit or Centigrade units, the reading literacy scores could just as easily have been placed on scales with other means and standard deviations.

Students who scored close to the international mean score of 500 were typically those who responded correctly to items which were of intermediate difficulty. For instance, they responded correctly to items which required processes like the following:

Narrative scale

    Can read a story about a shark which befriends a family of sardines and say why the shark was swimming alone.

    Can read a short fable about an elephant which was bothering a family of birds and say how the mother bird got the elephant to go away.

Expository scale

    Can read a short passage about quicksand, and respond correctly to a question which asks how to recognize quicksand.

    Can read a description of the walrus and say how long it lives as stated in the passage.

Documents scale

    Can study a simple map and identify the place south of point x.

    Can study a school timetable and work out which was the third lesson on Thursday.

Students who earned scores over 600 were able to respond correctly to very difficult items requiring the ability to read long complex stories or complicated figures and to make inferences about major themes, the motives of characters, or unusual relationships in the information given.

Students who scored below 400 had very limited reading ability. Typically they could respond correctly only on short simple passages where the items required limited processing or the answer was clearly stated in the passage.

More detailed information about the meaning of the scores will be presented in later publications. Further information about the rationale for the scores used in this booklet is provided in Appendix C.

Example: FINLAND Narrative scores

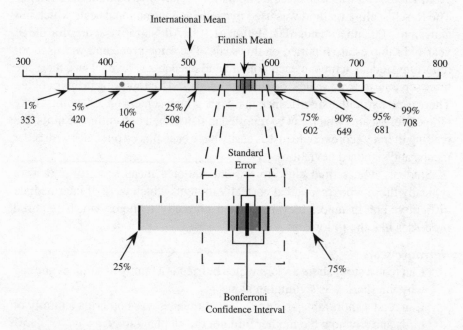

Interpreting the figures

Figures 3.1, 3.2, and 3.3 (at the end of this chapter) present the Population A reading literacy achievement results. In order to explain how to read Figures 3.1 to 3.3, an example is given above. It shows the results of FINLAND for the Narrative domain and is the same as that given on the first line of Figure 3.1. The left-hand vertical line represents the first percentile. For FINLAND this is 353. This is the score below which one percent of the sample scores. The dot at the left hand side is the score for the fifth percentile. This is the score (420) below which five percent of the sample of FINLAND performed. The next vertical line indicates the tenth percentile point, i.e., the score (466) below which ten percent of the sample scored. The 25th percentile (508) follows. The heavy black bar (at 500) is the international mean (average) score for all students in the survey. In the middle of the distribution, the long thin bar (at 568) is the mean score for the

Finnish sample on the Narrative domain items. Moving further to the right along the graph, the next vertical line is the 75th percentile (602), then the 90th percentile (649), the dot represents the 95th percentile (681), and the final bar the 99th percentile (708), i.e., the score below which 99 percent of the students in the FINLAND sample performed.

The middle section of the graph has been enlarged so that its parts can be seen. On either side of the Finnish mean there are two shaded areas. The darker (inner) area represents the standard error of sampling, i.e., the interval within which the actual average score lies (with 95 percent confidence). This interval extends plus or minus 6.0 (562-574) points from the mean. The lighter (outer) shaded area represents the Bonferroni confidence interval (558-579). The Bonferroni significance testing procedure is recommended when multiple comparisons are being made. In brief, it is a method of adjusting significance levels so that the probability of falsely rejecting one or more null hypotheses when many comparisons are made is kept to a fixed level.

Figure 3.4 shows the same means again, presented in the order of each nation's Composite Developmental Index (CDI). The CDI score in this figure is the scaled score expected on the basis of the CDI. Thus, SWITZERLAND, with a high CDI value of 4.29 (see Table 2.1) produces a high expected overall average score of 541. The actual mean domain scores for SWITZERLAND, shown in Figure 3.4, are 506, 507 and 522 for Narrative, Expository and Documents scales respectively. The figure shows which countries scored above and below the CDI prediction in each domain, and by how much.

A study of Figure 3.4 shows that the profile (performance on each of the domains) of most systems of education is relatively homogeneous across the three domains. If Population A students in a country are reading well according to the Narrative Scale, they are likely to be reading well in the other two scales also. Prominent exceptions to the rule of a homogeneous profile are DENMARK, HONG KONG and the two GERMANYS, which showed greater strength on the Documents Scale, and GREECE and INDONESIA, whose students were stronger on Narrative and Expository reading. While individual students within countries may have irregular profiles across the three types of reading literacy, the correlations between national means were very high at both age levels. Hence, there is justification for combining the domain scores for some purposes.

Table 3.1 presents the actual mean scores for all countries by separate domains and by an overall average of the three domain scores. It can be seen that the differences between most of the developed countries are not very great. Thus, 15 countries showed overall mean scaled scores between 500 and 540. There is a clustering of many education systems at this point on the scale. Nevertheless, there were a few countries which showed consistently high patterns of achievement across all domains at both age levels. Likewise, a few countries showed consistently low levels of literacy on each domain at both age levels. There is a stability in these patterns which is reflected in a high correlation between the mean national scores at the two age levels (0.83). There are real, stable differences in reading literacy levels between nations. Such differences give rise to interesting questions for research.

A few countries in Population A tested many underage or overage children. Thus, the average age for CANADA (BC) was 8.9 years, whereas the average age

Table 3.1. Mean student ability scores (with standard errors of sampling) for all domains, arranged in order of overall achievement: Population A

Country	Grade tested	Mean Age (in years)	Overall Mean (s.e.)	SD	Narrative Mean (s.e.)	SD	Expository Mean (s.e.)	SD	Documents Mean (s.e.)	SD
Finland	3	9.7	569	70	568 (3.0)	83	569 (3.1)	81	569 (4.0)	88
United States	4	10.0	547	74	553 (3.1)	96	538 (2.6)	80	550 (2.7)	81
Sweden	3	9.8	539	94	536 (2.6)	100	542 (2.7)	112	539 (3.2)	106
France	4	10.1	531	74	532 (4.1)	93	533 (4.1)	84	527 (3.9)	81
Italy	4	9.9	529	80	533 (4.0)	88	538 (4.0)	95	517 (4.9)	92
New Zealand	5	10.0	528	86	534 (3.5)	102	531 (3.1)	93	521 (3.3)	92
Norway	3	9.8	524	91	525 (2.8)	102	528 (2.3)	103	519 (2.8)	101
Iceland†	3	9.8	518	85	518 (0.0)	95	517 (0.0)	101	519 (0.0)	91
Hong Kong	4	10.0	517	71	494 (4.1)	87	503 (3.4)	72	554 (4.2)	89
Singapore	3	9.3	515	72	521 (1.1)	91	519 (1.0)	75	504 (1.0)	78
Switzerland	3	9.7	511	83	506 (2.6)	92	507 (2.7)	100	522 (2.8)	96
Ireland	4	9.3	509	79	518 (3.7)	94	514 (3.2)	89	495 (3.8)	84
Belgium/Fr	4	9.8	507	77	510 (3.3)	92	505 (2.8)	85	506 (3.5)	88
Greece	4	9.3	504	75	514 (3.8)	88	511 (3.6)	85	488 (3.8)	85
Spain	4	10.0	504	78	497 (2.4)	86	505 (2.3)	92	509 (2.7)	89
Germany/W	3	9.4	503	84	491 (2.8)	93	497 (2.9)	104	520 (3.2)	94
Canada/BC	3	8.9	500	80	502 (3.5)	96	499 (2.7)	94	500 (2.8)	86
Germany/E	3	9.5	499	84	482 (4.2)	93	493 (3.6)	103	522 (5.0)	96
Hungary	3	9.3	499	78	496 (2.9)	80	493 (3.1)	101	509 (3.5)	89
Slovenia	3	9.7	498	78	502 (2.7)	94	489 (2.5)	93	503 (2.5)	82
Netherlands	3	9.2	485	73	494 (3.3)	85	480 (3.4)	87	481 (3.9)	82
Cyprus	4	9.8	481	77	492 (2.4)	92	475 (2.3)	91	476 (2.1)	81
Portugal	4	10.4	478	74	483 (3.3)	81	480 (3.0)	84	471 (4.5)	92
Denmark	3	9.8	475	111	463 (3.4)	119	467 (3.5)	127	496 (3.6)	125
Trinidad/ Tobago	4	9.6	451	79	455 (3.6)	91	458 (3.4)	93	440 (3.3)	82
Indonesia	4	10.8	394	59	402 (2.8)	66	411 (3.2)	77	369 (3.0)	66
Venezuela	4	10.1	383	74	378 (3.2)	86	396 (3.3)	91	374 (3.7)	84

†Iceland tested all students, therefore no standard error was calculated.
s.e. = 1 standard error of sampling

in all countries tested was close to 9.7 years. Likewise, FRANCE, PORTUGAL, INDONESIA and VENEZUELA had large numbers of students over ten years of age. As these countries were 'outliers' in this respect, a fair comparison of their performance levels calls for some adjustment. However, there is no ideal method of arriving at such an adjustment from a cross-sectional survey. (See Appendix E on age adjustments.)

Not only are mean scores of interest, but much can be gleaned about the performance of the top and bottom 25 percent of students. For example, a perusal of Figure 3.1 (Narrative domain) would indicate that the top 25 percent in the UNITED STATES does particularly well, whereas in HUNGARY these students would appear to perform less well. The same can be said about PORTUGAL. It is also clear from Figure 3.1 that the bottom 25 percent in SWEDEN, NORWAY and CANADA (BC) perform less well than the bottom 25 percent in most other countries.

High Scoring Countries

It is clear from Figures 3.1 to 3.4 and from Table 3.1 that the 9-year-olds of FINLAND are the best readers on all three dimensions of reading literacy assessed in this survey with the highest average scores for each domain (Narrative 568, Expository 569, Documents 569). These scores are more than half a standard deviation above the international mean, and the average score is 20 points above the average score of the next country. Furthermore, Finnish students performed the best or second best on 70 percent of the 60 test items, and only 1 percent of students scored below a raw score of 25 percent, which is a crude but useful external indication of non-reading status on items which could be guessed correctly 25 percent of the time. What is most remarkable about this result is that children in FINLAND do not begin formal schooling until age seven, whereas in most of the remaining countries students begin to read at age six or younger. There is clearly something to be learned from the impressive way in which Finnish students acquire literacy – from their policies, their methods of instruction, and their attitudes to reading. This result also raises afresh the question of whether the consistent sound-symbol relationship of the Finnish language is a key factor in learning to read. The Finnish orthography is a highly regular system, which could well facilitate a child's passage into literacy (Kyöstiö 1980, Oney and Goldman 1984).

A comparison with the CDI (Figure 3.4) shows that FINLAND exceeded the average score that would be predicted by the nation's social and economic circumstances by a substantial margin (average, 39 points). These results are compatible with the Finnish performance on the Population B test. All the indications are consistent and stable. Finnish students are clearly very good readers by age nine.

The UNITED STATES also performed well above expectation (30 points above the CDI prediction) and had the second best outcome in the Narrative and Expository domains (553 and 538 respectively). The average score for reading literacy was consistent with the earlier IEA reading survey of 15 countries (Thorndike 1973). A close analysis of the American students' distribution shows consistently high performance on all items, and less than two percent of students scoring below the chance level cutoff point of 25 percent. Students in the American sample are relatively strong in literacy, in spite of reading in a language with an irregular orthography.

With a very high status on the CDI, the SWEDISH students were expected to achieve well. The results confirm this prediction with average scores on each domain close to 540 points (536, 542, 539). As in the other Scandinavian countries, they enjoy small classes and well-trained teachers but, like FINLAND, their students have been attending school only since age seven. As in the 1970 IEA survey and the pilot study of 1990, SWEDISH students showed a consistently high level of performance at this age level and have achieved close to their high CDI prediction. They too must have some lessons for reading educators in other countries.

FRANCE, NEW ZEALAND and ITALY have very similar profiles to that of SWEDEN. The absence of private schools in the French sample has an unknown influence on these results as well as on the CDI comparisons, but the state schools achieved above expectation by 21 points overall. The number below chance level was less than two percent.

NEW ZEALAND students also showed high standards in all domains and, relative to their more modest economic and social circumstances, were well above prediction (28 points). NEW ZEALAND reading methods have enjoyed a notable reputation internationally in view of their students' strong performance in the earlier IEA surveys of reading and literature. The fact that NEW ZEALAND students begin school at age five could well give them a favorable start in a survey of 9-year-olds, as these students were tested in a higher grade than were many others. However, the lack of relationship between the age of beginning instruction and performance is already becoming clear and will be examined more systematically later.

The 9-year-olds of ITALY scored at a similar level to NEW ZEALAND and their results were certainly consistent with a high level of performance in the Thorndike survey. Interestingly, they too have the advantage of a language which is phonetically very regular, which may facilitate the acquisition of literacy.

Other countries whose students scored above the international mean were NORWAY, ICELAND and HONG KONG, all with overall average scores close to 520 points. HONG KONG'S results were higher than anticipated, as its level of economic and social development is more modest than that of many of the countries in the survey, and their students were acquiring literacy in Chinese, a language with an ideographic script widely believed to present more difficulties for its students than the alphabetic script. The profile for HONG KONG students is intriguing, as they scored very high in the Documents scale (554, second highest), but only at or below the international mean in the Narrative (494) and Expository (503) domains. This pattern was strengthened by an analysis of their chance level scores. Less than one percent of HONG KONG 9-year-olds fell below 25 percent in the Documents scale, while over six percent did so on the Narrative scale. Variations in cultural emphasis and test taking traditions may account for these deviations.

NORWAY and ICELAND had very similar CDI predictions, very similar domain score levels (NORWAY 525, 528, 519; ICELAND 518, 517, 519) and very similar percentages of low scoring students. In both countries, formal instruction starts at age seven, the languages have similar degrees of phonetic regularity and they report similarly low numbers of hours of instruction per year. In both cases the students achieved at levels a little below what their high CDI status would predict.

CANADA (BC) students start school at six, but were tested in Grade 3, so their sample was nearly 10 months younger than the international mean age. However, even without an adjustment for age their students achieved close to the overall average of 9-year-olds, indicating a high level of literacy in the junior classes of British Columbia. SWITZERLAND also produced scores above the international average in all domains, and a particularly strong average score in the Documents scale (522).

Other countries well above expectation

Three other countries with mean achievement levels well above the levels predicted by their economic and social circumstances were SINGAPORE, HUNGARY, and SPAIN.

The case of SINGAPORE is particularly interesting as it is an example of a country where the language of instruction, and of testing, is different from that of the home for over 70 percent of the students. SINGAPORE children begin reading instruction in English at age six, yet most of them arrive at school speaking only their native Chinese or Malay or Tamil languages. The fact that the SINGAPORE students scored 521 and 519 in the Narrative and Expository domains must challenge the conventional wisdom that students should learn to read first in the language of the home. Like the students of HONG KONG, they showed very low numbers of students scoring below chance level on Documents (1.6 percent), but considerably more on Narrative (5.9 percent). The SINGAPORE education system must have some lessons for those schools and systems where students are acquiring literacy in a non-native language.

Two European countries with mean achievement levels above expectation were HUNGARY and SPAIN. Again one could point to the fact that, like FINLAND, both countries have a language which enjoys a high degree of regularity between grapheme and phoneme. This matter is examined more thoroughly in Chapter Five.

Countries With Relatively Low Achievement

As noted earlier, all the developing countries tended to have lower achievement levels than the industrialized nations. In general, their economic position is weaker and they lack long-standing literacy traditions. VENEZUELAN and INDO-NESIAN students had similarly low means in each subtest (378, 396, 374 and 402, 411, 369 respectively, or 35 percent to 40 percent correct). Nearly a third of the students in each country scored at chance levels or below, indicating virtual non-reader status. The results of the Word Recognition Test confirmed these findings. Moreover, the mean ages of the students sampled werehigher than in the other systems (10.7 and 10.8 years old, respectively). However, a closer analysis shows that the highest 25 percent of students in each country had more than half the items correct in each domain. It should be noted that for nearly 80 percent of INDONESIAN students the national language is their second or third language.

Another country with a low achievement level was TRINIDAD AND TOBAGO, with scaled score averages close to 450 (near 50 percent) in each domain. Nearly 15 percent of these 9-year-olds scored below 25 percent, yet they have been in school since age five. Government resources for education are relatively meager, but literacy levels do not reflect the current social and economic conditions as judged by the performance of 9-year-olds elsewhere. The average score overall was 26 points below CDI prediction.

Of the remaining countries, results in CYPRUS, PORTUGAL and DENMARK, with average scores below the international mean in each domain, revealed many struggling readers at this age. The discrepancy between the CDI prediction and the measured achievement level for DENMARK was surprising (-41 points) and out of line with that of the Danish 14-year-olds. A large number of Danish 9-year-olds failed to finish the tests, and as many as 17 percent scored below chance level. Danish students also attained low average scores and low comple-tion rates on the Word Recognition Test. Among the possible reasons for these results are the following: Danish students begin reading instruction only at age seven and at age nine they are quite unaccustomed to taking formal tests, according to the teachers' questionnaire responses. It was noted that many student showed a reluctance to answer when they were unsure.

The children of CYPRUS and PORTUGAL begin reading at ages five and six respectively, but both countries have a relatively low resource base for funding schools, below average adult literacy rates, and low preschool participation rates. Both had achievement means very close to their CDI expectation, which was below 500. The NETHERLANDS' result was also lower than anticipated but would be in line with prediction if an adjustment were made for the fact that the Dutch sample was considerably under age. (Such an adjustment is attempted in Appendix E.)

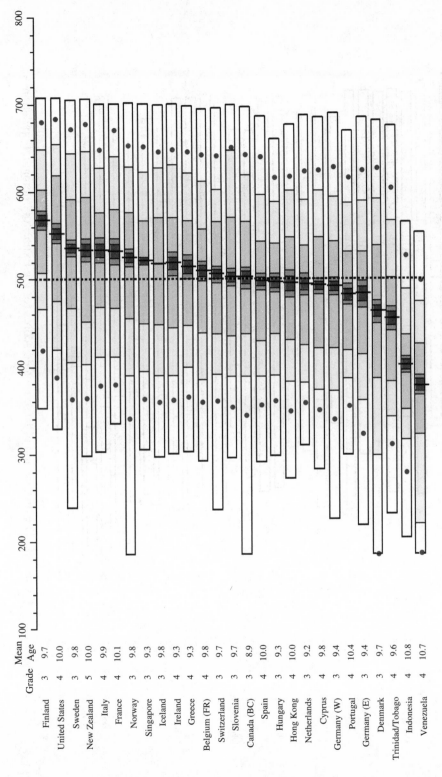

Figure 3.1. The distribution of Rasch scaled scores for the Narrative domain, Population A

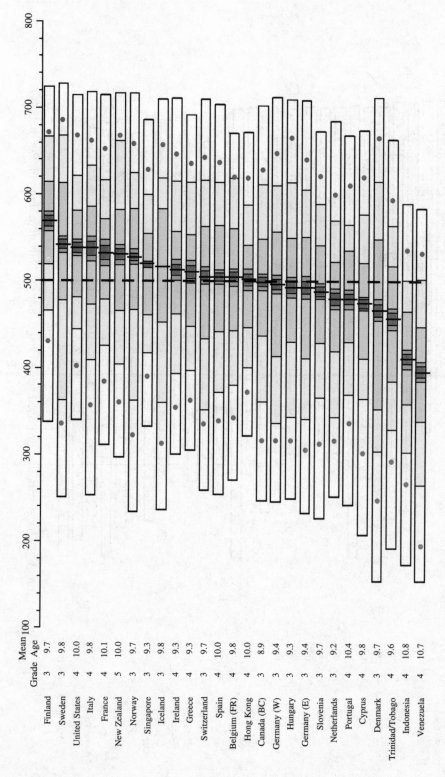

Figure 3.2. The distribution of Rasch scaled scores for the Expository domain, Population A

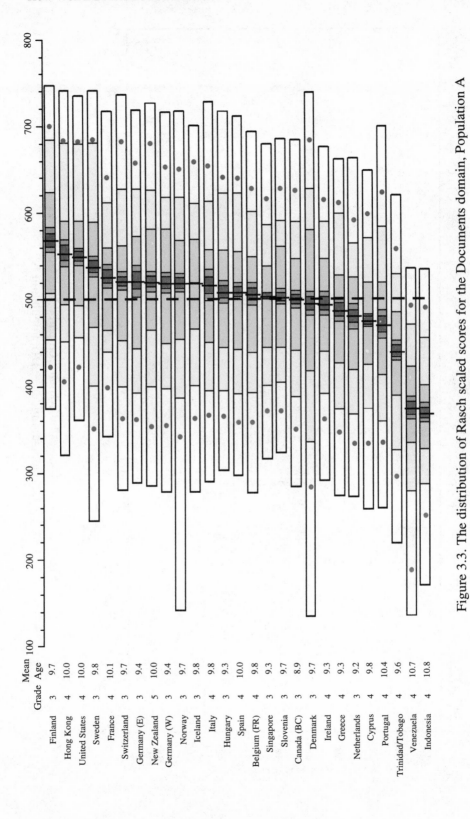

Figure 3.3. The distribution of Rasch scaled scores for the Documents domain, Population A

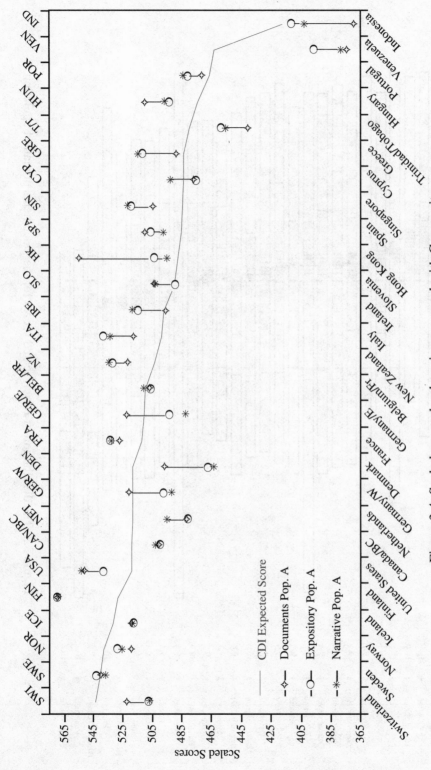

Figure 3.4. Scaled scores by domain compared with Composite.
Development Index (CDI), Population A

CHAPTER FOUR

HOW WELL DO FOURTEEN-YEAR-OLDS READ
AROUND THE WORLD?

General Comments

As in Population A, each of the domain scales for Population B has a mean of 500 and a standard deviation of 100. However, the reading ability required to gain a score of 500 is greater than that required for a score of 500 on the Population A scales.

Students who scored approximately 500 on the Population B scales were typically able to respond correctly to items which required abilities such as the following:

Narrative scale

Given a story about a magician whose audience suspected him of having many things up his sleeve, students can infer the magician's feelings.

Given a story about a young man who killed a fox he came upon unexpectedly, students can say what the writer's message was.

Expository scale

Given a lengthy magazine article on the development of the laser, students can identify what was its most spectacular success.

Given a descriptive passage about a family of marmots, students can infer why the grass in the area is healthy.

Documents scale

Given a chart listing weather conditions in 40 cities, students can determine what was the low temperature in city X.

Given a map, students can use its legend to identify what resources are found in region X.

At the upper levels, students who gained scores over 600 were able to comprehend long complex passages with a heavy vocabulary load well enough to respond correctly to questions which require subtle inferences or to integrate information from different parts of the passage. Students who scored below the 400 level were able to read short to medium length passages well enough to respond correctly to questions about facts given in the passage or to make easy inferences about them.

Figures 4.1 to 4.3 present the achievement results for each domain in the Population B tests, arranged in order of overall performance level, and Figure 4.4 presents the same results, arranged in order of the countries' Composite Developmental Index (CDI). Table 4.1 presents the average scores. Nigeria, Thailand and Zimbabwe had response rates below 80 percent, and are marked with asterisks. Also, France, Portugal and Venezuela had considerably overage samples. Adjustments for age would reduce their scores by 15 to 20 points, and raise those of CANADA (BC) by a similar margin. Caution should be exercised in judging the performance levels of these seven countries.

Table 4.1. Mean student ability scores (with standard errors of sampling) for all domains arranged in order of overall achievement: Population B.

Country	Grade tested	Mean age (in years)	Overall Mean (s.e.)	SD	Narrative Mean (s.e.)	SD	Expository Mean (s.e.)	SD	Documents Mean (s.e.)	SD
Finland	8	14.7	560	65	559 (2.8)	84	541 (2.2)	71	580 (2.5)	82
France	9	15.4	549	68	556 (4.2)	86	546 (4.3)	84	544 (4.2)	77
Sweden	8	14.8	546	80	556 (2.6)	93	533 (2.4)	91	550 (2.4)	90
New Zealand	10	15.0	545	92	547 (5.7)	104	535 (5.7)	105	552 (5.3)	98
Hungary	8	14.1	536	73	530 (3.1)	81	536 (3.6)	91	542 (3.2)	82
Iceland	8	14.8	536	78	550 (0.0)	91	548 (0.0)	100	509 (0.0)	77
Switzerland	8	14.9	536	74	534 (3.4)	90	525 (3.2)	87	549 (3.0)	82
Hong Kong	9	15.2	535	64	509 (3.7)	72	540 (3.8)	79	557 (3.8)	76
United States	9	15.0	535	85	539 (4.9)	98	539 (5.6)	107	528 (4.0)	84
Singapore	8	14.4	534	66	530 (1.1)	73	539 (1.2)	82	533 (1.1)	74
Slovenia	8	14.7	532	63	534 (2.6)	76	525 (2.2)	73	537 (2.2)	74
Germany/E	8	14.4	526	73	512 (3.9)	90	523 (3.5)	87	543 (2.9)	81
Denmark	8	14.8	525	77	517 (2.0)	83	524 (2.2)	94	532 (2.1)	88
Portugal	9	15.6	523	60	523 (2.5)	71	523 (3.4)	79	523 (3.4)	67
Canada/BC	8	13.9	522	81	526 (3.1)	94	516 (3.1)	97	522 (2.7)	88
Germany/W	8	14.6	522	78	514 (4.9)	95	521 (4.5)	92	532 (3.9)	82
Norway	8	14.8	516	71	515 (2.1)	76	520 (2.4)	86	512 (2.4)	82
Italy	8	14.1	515	73	520 (3.6)	88	524 (3.2)	85	501 (3.3)	78
Netherlands	8	14.3	514	76	506 (4.8)	88	503 (4.7)	83	533 (5.3)	90
Ireland	9	14.5	511	81	510 (5.3)	93	505 (5.3)	94	518 (4.9)	90
Greece	9	14.4	509	65	526 (2.9)	75	508 (3.1)	84	493 (2.6)	69
Cyprus	9	14.8	497	73	516 (2.2)	82	492 (2.4)	91	482 (2.0)	74
Spain	8	14.2	490	65	500 (3.0)	84	495 (2.6)	79	475 (2.0)	64
Belgium/Fr	8	14.3	481	78	484 (5.1)	95	477 (4.8)	89	483 (4.7)	82
Trinidad/ Tobago	9	14.4	479	87	482 (1.7)	96	485 (1.8)	100	472 (1.7)	92
Thailand*	9	15.2	477	79	468 (6.6)	88	486 (5.9)	87	478 (6.2)	88
Philippines	8	14.5	430	65	421 (3.6)	71	439 (4.1)	78	430 (3.9)	72
Venezuela	9	15.5	417	61	407 (2.9)	67	433 (3.3)	80	412 (3.0)	70
Nigeria†*	9	15.3	401	65	402 (---)	69	406 (---)	73	394 (---)	81
Zimbabwe*	9	15.5	372	60	367 (3.3)	64	374 (3.6)	70	373 (4.6)	83
Botswana	7	14.7	330	43	340 (1.6)	53	339 (1.9)	58	312 (2.4)	69

† Insufficient data to calculate the Design Effect.

* Sampling response rates of schools was below 80 percent.

s.e. = 1 standard error of sampling

At the Population B level there is again a group of countries in the 500 to 540 range whose between-country differences are remarkably similar to those of Population A. For those countries participating in both populations the correlation between average scores for the two age groups is 0.83. While the differences between these countries are often not statistically significant (when the conservative Bonferroni Tests of Significance are applied), the relative performance levels are surprisingly stable across surveys taken at different ages and at different times.

High Achieving Countries: Population B

Once again, students of FINLAND achieved the highest average score of all countries in the Narrative and Documents domains, although they dropped a little in the Expository domain. A perusal of the item analysis results showed that they had the highest or second highest percentage of students with correct answers on approximately half of the items over all tests. There is no doubt that the Finnish students have maintained the position of their younger counterparts as the most competent readers of all countries in the survey. Their average score was also 18 points above expectation, based on their CDI.

Very high performance was shown also by the students of FRANCE with the second highest average score in the Narrative (556) and Expository (546) domains, and sixth highest in Documents (544). It should be remembered that this result applies only to French public schools (i.e., 75 percent of the total population of 14-year-olds). Moreover, they had a mean age of 15 years 5 months (9 months above the international mean age). Again, the average level achieved by the French sample was higher by 23 points than expected on the basis of the CDI.

SWEDEN and NEW ZEALAND also showed very high performance levels. SWEDEN's result, like that of FINLAND, is notable because it was achieved by students with fewer years at school and fewer hours of instruction than most. NEW ZEALAND students scored above their expected average score by 32 points, though not as well as in the 1970 survey (Thorndike 1973).

SWITZERLAND's 14-year-olds had an excellent result on the Documents scale (549), but were less successful in the Expository domain (525). Two other countries showing high performance, relative to expectation and age were HUNGARY and SLOVENIA. On the CDI, HUNGARY ranks only 22nd, but their students' reading literacy means were in the top nine for each domain. The average score was 57 points above prediction. HUNGARIAN students have raised their performance level since the last IEA Reading Study (Thorndike 1973) and now read relatively well in all areas. At a similar level was SLOVENIA (534, 525, 537), which exceeded expectation by 32 points. ICELANDIC students showed an unusually strong performance on the Expository scale (548 the highest mean), but were less successful in their level of Document literacy (509).

SINGAPORE students, like their younger counterparts, performed very well in the Narrative and Expository domains (530 and 539 respectively). Again, the notable point to remember about this result is that SINGAPORE 14-year-olds have English as their medium of instruction and testing from the first year of school, yet it is the home language of only 26 percent of the sample. As at the 9-year-old level, SINGAPORE students achieved well above expectation (43 points) based on their economic and social circumstances and on linguistic considerations. They were also below the international average in age.

HONG KONG students showed an impressive profile in the Document and Expository scales (557, 540) but dropped quite steeply in the Narrative section (509). Their unusual profile across domains was similar to that of the 9-year-olds, suggesting that it is not unique to one set of reading exercises. However, it should be noted that the HONG KONG sample was nearly five months older than the international mean age. It is also worthy of comment that HONG KONG and SINGAPORE were among the top five countries in the extent to which they achieved above expectation, relative to their CDI prediction. While both countries are populated largely by Chinese students, their schooling is conducted in languages that could not be more different.

Also listed in this group of high-achieving countries was the UNITED STATES, with domain scores that clustered around 535, and an overall performance level very close to the level expected by their level of economic and social development. It will be noted that the American students performed considerably better at the 9-year-old level relative to the other participating countries than at the 14-year-old level.

Countries with relatively low achievement

As at the 9-year-old level, the 14-year-olds in developing countries fared less well in their levels of reading literacy in all domains. Students in BOTSWANA, NIGERIA and ZIMBABWE scored at or below 400 points, and each had large numbers of students below the *chance level* mark of 25 percent. In all three cases, the majority of the students were tested in a non-native language, and the resource levels and traditions of literacy in each case were less than favorable.

The 14-year-olds in VENEZUELA and the PHILIPPINES performed somewhat better with their literacy tasks, showing average scores of 417 (407, 433, 412) and 430 (421, 439, 430) respectively, but the VENEZUELAN achievement level was still well below expectation. Furthermore, only 72 percent of their 14-year-olds were still in school. THAILAND had relatively higher means (468, 486, 478), but it has only 33 percent of this age group in school. TRINIDAD AND TOBAGO students achieved at a much higher level at age fourteen than at age nine and had average scores within 20 points of the international average, almost up to their predicted level across domains.

Among the European countries results of the students in BELGIUM (FR) and the NETHERLANDS were lower than expected. They fell below CDI prediction by 39 and 17 points respectively. Both countries had large numbers of students younger than 14.5 years at the time of testing, but an adjustment for age would only raise their estimated scores by approximately ten points. PORTUGAL showed much better performance levels at age fourteen than at age nine, but it should be noted that their students were 15.6 years old at the time of testing.

Distribution of Scores

Again, the reader may well wish to peruse Figures 4.1, 4.2 and 4.3 for performance at different parts of the score distributions. For instance, the range of scores for PORTUGAL and SINGAPORE in each domain is narrow; for NEW ZEALAND the scores are widely distributed. It can be seen that the top five percent of students are very similar in their performance levels in Narrative for the first 25 countries, but more variable in the other two domains. Also the contrast in performance levels between the developing countries and the remaining countries is apparent at all points in the distribution for each domain.

A study of Figure 4.4 reveals other trends. The students of PORTUGAL produced the same mean score in each domain; those of FINLAND and HONG KONG clear differences between domains. Students of FRANCE, NEW ZEALAND, SINGAPORE, HUNGARY and PORTUGAL achieved consistently well above the scores predicted by their CDI; those of NORWAY, BELGIUM (FR), ZIMBABWE and BOTSWANA performed consistently below theirs.

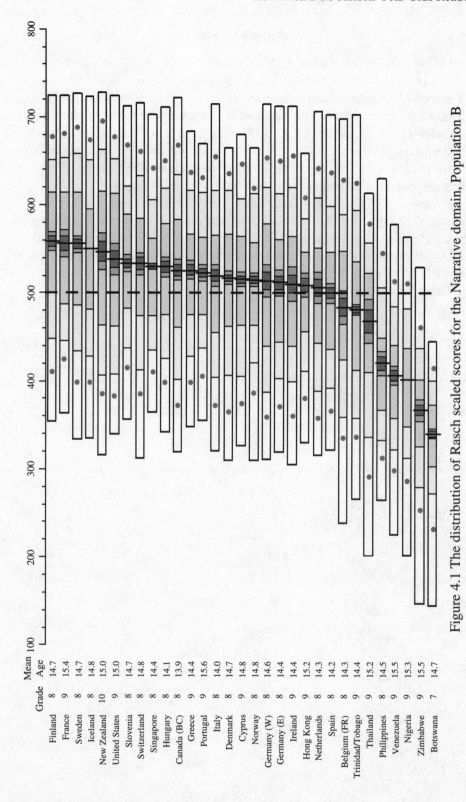

Figure 4.1 The distribution of Rasch scaled scores for the Narrative domain, Population B

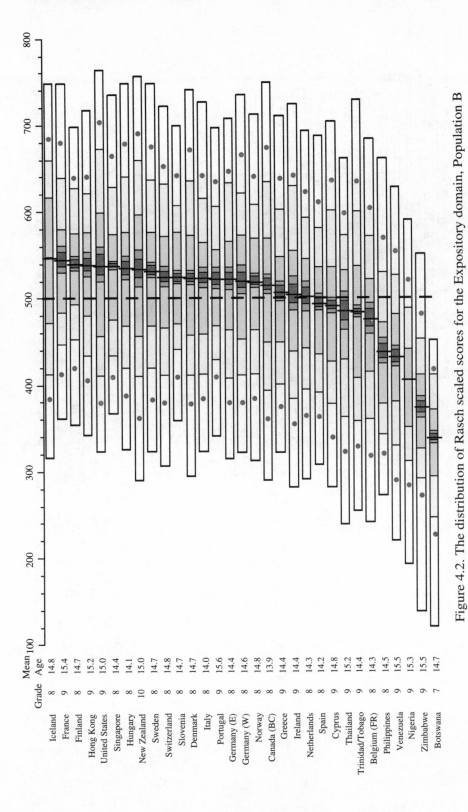

Figure 4.2. The distribution of Rasch scaled scores for the Expository domain, Population B

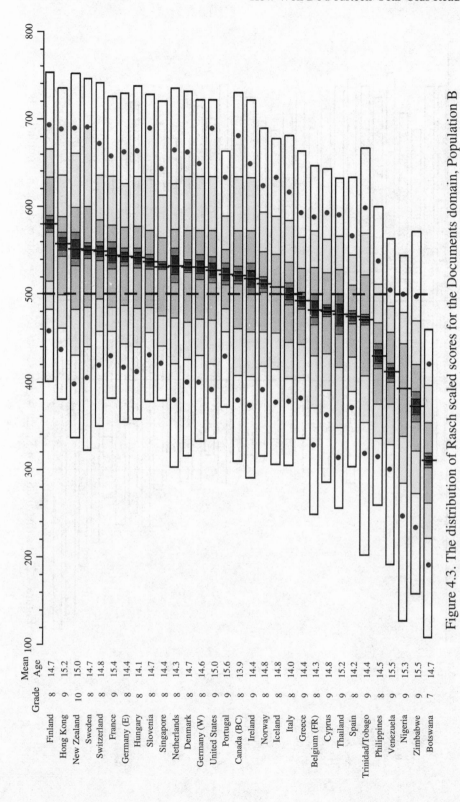

Figure 4.3. The distribution of Rasch scaled scores for the Documents domain, Population B

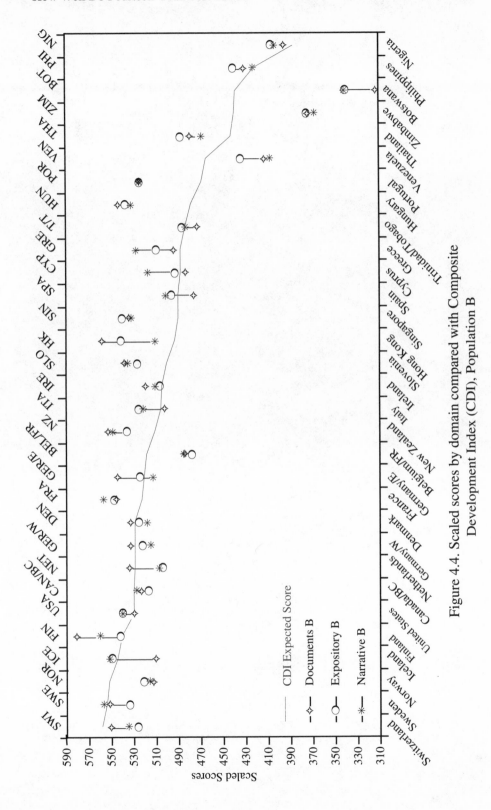

Figure 4.4. Scaled scores by domain compared with Composite Development Index (CDI), Population B

CHAPTER FIVE

HOW DO HIGH-ACHIEVING COUNTRIES DIFFER FROM LOW-ACHIEVING COUNTRIES?

A question often asked of those who conduct cross-national studies is: What brings about these differences in achievement levels between nations? Why, for instance did FINLAND's students achieve so well, relative to other nation's standards? What brought about the unusual profile of results in HONG KONG? Are such differences caused by educational policies or are they attributable to a variety of wider cultural and economic factors? What can be learned from a scrutiny of the results so far? Correlation studies cannot reveal causes. However, comparison between high- and low-scoring countries can identify factors which deserve closer study, and those which are unlikely to be important.

To pursue this question, the countries were arranged in order of average achievement scores, across all domains, and relevant indicators of hypothesized causes and correlates of high achievement were collected from the Student, Teacher and School Principal Questionnaires, the National Case Study Questionnaire and from other sources such as Unesco and World Bank Reports. These indicators were grouped into two categories for closer analysis.

1. *General:* Those which are indicative of the general level of social and economic development in each country, and largely beyond the control of educators; and
2. *Educational:* Those which are indicators of educational policies, and practices.

General Influences on School and Community Literacy Levels

The rationale for each of the chosen variables is given briefly. Many of these general influences are identical to those included in the CDI.

1. *GNP Per Capita (US$).* Wealthy nations can afford to put more resources into education.
2. *Adult Literacy.* High levels of adult literacy in a society suggest a greater societal pressure to acquire literacy in the next generation.
3. *Newspaper Circulation (per 1000 people).* More newspapers are a sign of the community's wish to keep abreast of world events by means of reading. Again, this reflects a societal pressure to read.
4. *Public Library Books (per 1000 people).* An abundance of books in libraries is another index of the extent to which citizens emphasize reading as a pursuit, and provide opportunities for young people to read.

5. *Economic Status of Teachers.* Where teachers are accorded high status, the profession is more likely to attract bright young people into teaching, which should in turn enhance the quality of education. This factor was estimated by comparing average teacher salaries with those of police, nurses and bus-drivers, as estimated by National Research Coordinators.
6. *Expenditure on Education, Per Student (US$).* The amount spent on schooling is an index of the value placed on children's education in the society, as well as another index of wealth.
7. *Language Homogeneity of Sample.* If there are many students whose home language is different from that of the school, the achievement levels in literacy in that language would be expected to be lower.
8. *Low Birth Weight Infants.* The percentage of infants born in the official *Low Birth Weight* category is an indicator of the health and welfare of mothers and children, and thus an indirect measure of the learning potential of students.
9. *Life Expectancy.* This is another index of the general health of the citizens of the country, and indirectly a probable influence on the effort which children can put into learning.

Table 5.1 lists the 31 systems for which data were available in Population B in order of mean scaled score across domains and the nine potential influences listed above. Based on available statistics, the countries were compared on each variable. Those that were in the top quarter of countries on a variable were recorded with a diamond; those in the second highest quarter of countries on that variable were recorded with a circle. The horizontal lines show how the countries cluster by score after taking into account the standard errors of sampling of those scores. For example, the seven countries with the highest *teacher economic status* are marked with a diamond in column one, and the seven countries with the highest *GNP per capita* are marked with a diamond in column five. In the *adult literacy* column (column 3), all fifteen countries reporting 99 percent adult literacy are marked with a diamond. The variables are arranged from the those least related to achievement (and therefore spread across most countries) to those which are increasingly limited to the higher achieving countries.

A study of Table 5.1 shows that the countries whose students were judged by the IEA tests to be most literate at age 14 are more advantaged on these nine criteria than those lower down the table. FINNISH and SWEDISH students, for instance, live in a rich, well educated, relatively homogeneous society with an abundance of literary resources, and high standards of health. The last three countries on the list, however, share virtually none of these apparently beneficial economic and social conditions. To some extent, literacy levels reflect economic and cultural advantages of the country as a whole.

Table 5.1. Relationships of national mean scores and school/community indicators: Population B.

	High teacher econ. status	High exp. on educ.	High adult lit.†	High life expect.	High GNP per cap.	Few low birth weight	High lang. homo-geneity	High public library hldgs.	High news-paper circ.
Finland	◊	°	◊	°	◊	◊	◊	◊	◊
France		°	◊	°	°	°	°		
Sweden	°	◊	◊	◊	◊	◊	°	◊	◊
New Zealand			◊	°		°	°	°	°
Switzerland	°	◊		◊	◊	°		°	◊
Iceland		°	◊	◊	°	◊	◊	◊	◊
Hungary			◊				◊		°
United States		◊	◊	°	◊		◊	◊	°
Hong Kong	◊		◊	◊					
Singapore	◊								°
Slovenia			◊						
Germany/East	°	°	◊		°		◊	◊	◊
Denmark	°	◊		°	◊		°	◊	◊
Portugal			◊				◊	°	
Germany/West	◊	◊	◊	°	◊	°			°
Canada/BC	°	◊		◊	°			°	°
Norway	°	◊	◊		◊	◊	°	°	◊
Italy			◊	◊	°				
Netherlands	◊	°		◊	°	◊			°
Ireland						◊	◊	°	
Greece				◊			°		
Cyprus	◊			°			°		
Spain	°			◊					
Belgium/Fr		°	◊	°	°	°			
Trinidad/Tobago		°							
Thailand									
Philippines									
Venezuela	◊								
Nigeria									
Zimbabwe									
Botswana									

Key: ◊ = In the top quarter of countries on this variable
      ° = In the second highest quarter of countries on this variable
      † = 15 countries reported 99% adult literacy

Nevertheless, the relationship is by no means perfect. FRANCE, NEW ZEALAND, HUNGARY, SINGAPORE, and HONG KONG achieved well above expectation on these counts, and a few wealthy European countries fell below theirs. There are clearly some educational factors which are exerting influences on achievement beyond these economic and cultural indicators.

Table 5.2 shows the disparities between the ten highest and lowest scoring countries in Population B. Thus, among the highest ten countries, five had *teacher economic status* in the top half of all countries. In the lowest scoring ten countries, three did. For newspaper circulation eight of the highest scoring countries had high newspaper circulation and none of the ten lowest scoring countries had this variable. Clearly, these nine variables can account for some of the differences between the achievement levels of the countries in this study. The correlation between national achievement means and CDI, which is based on six of these nine indicators is 0.76. Affluence, health and literacy pressures in the community are important.

Table 5.2. Comparison of high scoring and low scoring countries on development indicators for Population B.

	Highest 10 countries	Lowest 10 countries	Difference
Teacher economic status	5	3	2
Expenditure on education	6	2	4
Adult literacy	8	1	7
Life expectancy	8	3	5
GNP per capita	6	1	5
Low birth weight	6	1	5
Language homogeneity	7	1	6
Public library	6	0	6
Newspaper circulation	8	0	8

A similar pattern was observed in Population A, with slightly lower correlations. What is of greater interest to educators, however, is to investigate the relationship between the achievement levels and national educational policies. This exercise is reported first for Population A and is based on a contrast of the policies which are typical of high-scoring and of low-scoring countries.

Educational Policy Indicators: Population A

In order to investigate the influences of educational factors on national achievement levels, 21 educational policy indicators were selected. Each of these represented a policy which varied between countries, was readily available, was stable over time and has been the subject of debate among policymakers and researchers in many countries.

All the countries which participated in the Population A survey were listed in order of mean national achievement over all domains, ranging from age of beginning instruction to the frequency of formal testing. These figures were obtained from National Case Study Questionnaires, Teachers' Questionnaires and Unesco and World Bank Reports.

Table 5.3 summarizes these figures by comparing the average profiles of students in the ten highest- and lowest-scoring countries. The middle seven countries were not included in this analysis. The table presents the means for both groups of countries, the differences between these means and the differences expressed as a proportion of the standard deviation of all countries on that variable. In this table, any proportion over 0.30, that is, three-tenths of one standard deviation, is regarded as a sign of an important variable. This comparison provides some indication of the importance of each variable in reading literacy performance. However, in studying these figures, it must be remembered that much of the difference between these two sets of countries is probably attributable to differences in economic and social development, already observed. Some of these indicators may well be signs of affluence, without beneficial effects on literacy levels.

Such an analysis gives rise to another comparison, between those ten countries which exceeded their expected score by the most and those which fell most below the score expected on the basis of their CDI.* This analysis is presented in Table 5.4.

What do these comparisons reveal about the importance of these educational indicators in reading literacy achievement?

1. *Starting age of reading instruction.* Four countries start formal teaching of reading at age five, while eight systems start at age seven. Does the latter group show any disadvantage from the later start? Not according to Table 5.3. The ten highest-scoring countries began instruction at mean age of 6.3 years, and the lowest ten only 5.9 years. FINLAND, SWEDEN, NORWAY and ICELAND begin instruction at age seven, yet the nine-year-olds in these four countries surprisingly all fell in the top ten countries. However, all four countries are also in the top group on the CDI index, so they may have done well regardless of the age of beginning instruction. How does this variable appear in Table 5.4, after the adjustment for differences in economic and social development? This time the pattern is reversed. Four of the countries which started at age seven were in the lowest ten in relation to CDI prediction, and there is a margin of 0.45 years, favoring an earlier start. This represents a difference of 0.69 of a standard deviation. At age nine, there is still some advantage for an earlier start, but it can be said that countries which begin instruction in reading at age seven have largely caught up with the five- and six-year-old starters in reading ability by age nine.

---

* It will be remembered that the Composite Development Index (CDI) is made up of six equally weighted factors: per capita GNP, educational expenditure per student, life expectancy, percent low birth weight infants, newspaper circulation per 100, and adult literacy.

Table 5.3. Relative importance of selected national policy indicators in relation to national achievement means for Population A.

Policy indicator	Highest 10 countries	Lowest 10 countries	Diff / SD	Proportion of SD	Advantage for . . .
1 Starting age of instruction	6.3 yrs	5.9 yrs	0.40/0.65	0.62	Later start
2 % Students in pre-school	68.7	53.8	14.9/31.36	0.48	Preschool enrollment
3 Class size in sample	25.1	24.9	0.2/5.72	0.03	No difference
4 % Female teachers in sample	79.7	76.3	3.4/16.53	0.20	No difference
5 School days per year	178.9	191.6	12.7/19.08	0.67	Shorter year
6 Hours instruction per week	21.7	20.6	1.1/3.49	0.32	More hours instruction
7 Phonic regularity of language	2.6	3.2	0.6/1.21	0.50	Less regular language
8 % Multi-grade classes	20.3	24.4	3.1/23.2	0.18	No difference
9 Years teaching this class	1.57 yrs	1.56 yrs	0.01/0.60	0.02	No difference
10 Years teacher education	13.80	12.6	1.2/1.75	0.69	More education for teachers
11 % Other language speaking teachers	10.7	9.8	0.9/21.32	0.04	No difference
12 Easy access to books in community	74.2	62.0	12.2/15.2	0.80	Easy access to books
13 Size of school library	3.50	2.56	0.94/1.97	0.48	Large school library
14 Large classroom libraries	45.6	22.8	22.8/22.7	1.00	Large classroom library
15 Textbooks per student	1.74	1.59	0.15/0.47	0.32	More textbooks
16 Frequency borrow books from library	3.25	2.95	0.30/0.51	0.59	More books borrowed
17 Time on teaching the language	8.12 hrs	7.07 hrs	1.05/2.41	0.44	More time on language teaching
18 Frequency silent reading in class	3.43	3.36	0.09/0.93	0.08	No difference
19 Frequency teachers read to class	2.76	2.25	0.51/1.18	0.43	More teacher reading to class
20 % teachers give frequent reading tests	38.0	51.4	13.4/29.0	0.46	Fewer tests
21 Speed of word recognition	86.9	77.4	9.53/6.32	1.51	Faster word recognition

Table 5.4. Relative importance of selected national policy indicators for Population A after adjustment for economic and social conditions.

Policy indicator	Highest 10 countries	Lowest 10 countries	Diff / SD	Proportion of SD	Advantage for . . .
1 Starting age of instruction	5.95 yrs	6.40 yrs	0.45/0.64	0.69	Early start
2 % Students in pre-school	62.9	65.7	2.80/31.36	0.09	No difference
3 Class size in sample	27.63	23.7	3.93/5.72	0.69	Larger classes
4 % Female teachers in sample	78.4	71.8	6.6/16.5	0.40	More female teachers
5 School days per year	177.6	195.6	18.00/19.08	0.94	Shorter year
6 Hours instruction per week	22.8	19.7	2.2/3.49	0.60	More hours instruction
7 Phonic regularity of language	2.78	2.40	0.22/1.21	0.18	No difference
8 % Multi-grade classes	20.1	20.2	0.1/23.1	0.00	No difference
9 Years teaching this class	1.43 yrs	1.69 yrs	0.26/0.60	0.43	Fewer years with class
10 Years teacher education	13.9 yrs	13.2 yrs	0.7/1.75	0.40	More education for teachers
11 % Other language speaking teachers	12.0	10.7	1.3/21.1	0.06	No difference
12 Easy access to books in community	71.2	67.3	3.9/15.2	0.26	No difference
13 Size of school library	3.50	2.06	1.70/2.34	0.82	Large school library
14 Large classroom libraries	55.1	43.5	11.6/22.7	0.51	Larger classroom library
15 Textbooks per student	1.66	1.57	0.09/0.47	0.19	No difference
16 Frequency borrow books from library	3.06	2.90	0.16/0.51	0.31	More books borrowed
17 Time on teaching the language	7.95 hrs	6.67 hrs	1.28/2.41	0.53	More time on language teaching
18 Frequency silent reading in class	3.58	2.86	0.72/0.92	0.78	More silent reading
19 Frequency teachers read to class	2.59	2.30	0.29/1.18	0.25	No difference
20 % teachers give frequent reading tests	46.7	32.4	14.30/28.98	0.49	More frequent tests
21 Speed of word recognition	86.3	78.0	8.3/6.3	1.32	Faster word recognition

2.   *Pre-school enrollment rates.* Countries vary considerably in the extent to which they offer pre-school educational services. Several European countries enroll the complete cohort from age four or five; others report less than 25 percent participation at this level.

   The first analysis in Table 5.3 shows that the higher the enrollment ratio, the better the students' achievement at age nine. However, when adjusted for CDI, the pattern is reversed again, dropping to 0.09 standard deviation (See Table 5.4). It appears that attendance at pre-school has little effect on reading literacy levels at age nine, other things being equal. Of course, a closer analysis may reveal important differences in the content and quality of the programs offered, but it is noticeable that students of SINGAPORE and GREECE achieved well above expectation, yet less than a third of their cohorts attended pre-school institutions.

3.   *Size of class.* Small classes are preferred by most teachers, yet any reduction in the ratio of class teachers to pupils is an expensive policy, and researchers have not always provided clear-cut findings on its effectiveness. In this study, the class sizes varied from 16 or 17 in ITALY, NORWAY, and DENMARK, to 36 and 38 in HONG KONG and SINGAPORE. A straightforward comparison shows virtually no difference between high and low scoring countries. However, when adjustments were made for CDI, countries with larger classes fared better. The two Asian countries, SINGAPORE and HONG KONG, were outliers here. Without them the difference would disappear. Similar trends were found for Japan and Korea in earlier IEA studies (e.g., Postlethwaite and Wiley 1992).

4.   *Proportion of female teachers in the system.* Countries varied in the proportion of female teachers in their primary schools, from 98 percent in SLOVENIA to only 46 percent in INDONESIA. However, the two analyses were consistent in showing that high average reading scores were obtained in education systems with higher proportions of women teachers. While the difference was only 0.20 standard deviation in a straightforward contrast between high-scoring and low-scoring countries, it increased to 0.40 standard deviation when adjusted for CDI.

5.   *Number of official school days per annum.* The number of days a school is open to students is often debated as an important ingredient in raising achievement levels. While this may be true in some subjects, it appears to have no bearing on reading achievement. In fact the opposite is the case. In countries where schools are open for more than 190 days the achievement levels are generally lower than when they are open for less than 180 days. Indeed, some of the systems which produced the highest achievers, relative to expectation, required schools to be open for fewer than 170 days. This finding is counter-intuitive, and open to a variety of interpretations.

6. *Number of hours of instruction per week.* As the number of instructional hours per day varies across countries, a further check on the time students attend school was undertaken by counting the number of hours of instruction per week. This time there was a slight advantage for more hours in school, especially after adjusting for economic differences.

7. *Phonetic regularity of the language.* It is often claimed that languages which show a regular correspondence between sound and symbol make learning to read easier than those which have an irregular sound-letter correspondence. There is quite enough for the young child to remember without being confused by exceptions in the orthography. To check out this hypothesis, the 15 main European languages used in Population A were rated on a five point scale according to the extent to which their graphemes mapped faithfully on to their phonemes. The results of this exercise are shown in Table 5.5.

Table 5.5. Rating of languages according to phonetic regularity.

Highly Regular	5	Finnish
	4	Spanish, Italian, Portuguese, Hungarian, Slovenian
	3	German, Dutch, Swedish, Norwegian, Icelandic, Greek
	2	Danish, French
Irregular	1	English

Each country had these ratings applied according to its language of instruction, and comparisons were made between the high-scoring and low-scoring nations. While the FINNISH and ITALIAN students' results bore out the hypothesis of the benefits of regularity, the results of the remaining countries did not. The degree of regularity may be one factor which assists students when the sound-symbol link is near perfect, and the teaching methods exploit that fact, but it is apparently not a major consideration in other languages by age nine.

8. *Policy of educating children in multi-grade classrooms.* In NEW ZEALAND, PORTUGAL, and TRINIDAD AND TOBAGO, over 70 percent of teachers reported having multi-grade classes; in GERMANY, SINGAPORE, and SLOVENIA, none did. While this policy may generate beneficial effects for students in some subjects, there was no difference found in this study between high-scoring and low-scoring countries in the proportion of teachers with multi-grade classes before or after adjustment.

9. *Average number of years teachers have stayed with their present class.* Several European countries in this study have a policy of encouraging

teachers to stay with one class for several years. In ITALY, DENMARK, FRANCE and SWEDEN, most teachers reported that they had been with their present class for more than two years; in most remaining countries the average time was less than one year. Initial inspection showed no difference in this respect (Table 5.3), but in those countries where literacy performance was above expectation, the teachers had spent somewhat less time on average, with their present class (Table 5.4).

10. *Number of years teachers have spent acquiring their education.* AMERICAN teachers reported an average of 17.2 years of education, CANADIAN (BC) teachers 16.8 years, and NORWEGIAN teachers 16.6 years. By contrast, EAST GERMAN and DUTCH teachers had less than eleven years education. These figures include school, university and teacher training. The ten high-scoring countries reported 13.8 years on average, and the low-scoring countries only 12.6 years, which represents a substantial difference. Even after adjustment for economic and social circumstances the difference still favored a longer education (see Table 5.4).

11. *Percentage of teachers whose first language is different from that of the school.* Most countries employ some teachers whose first language is different from that of the school. In SINGAPORE (84 percent) and INDONESIA (78 percent) such teachers are in the majority. Only HUNGARY and PORTUGAL reported no such teachers. At this age, the difference is not large, either before or after the adjustment for economic conditions.

12. *Easy access to books in the community at large.* Many literacy surveys show access to books is related to reading ability. In this survey, principals were asked to report on whether the students had easy access to public libraries and to book-stores in the community, and students were asked to report on the number of books in the home. The percentage of students reporting over 100 books, was found to correlate highly with the other two access indicators, and as all had a similar variance they were combined into a single index. Best access was found in the NETHERLANDS (86 percent), SWITZERLAND (84 percent) and SWEDEN (83 percent); the worst in INDONESIA (22 percent), PORTUGAL (40 percent) and VENEZUELA (46 percent). Table 5.3 shows that high-scoring countries averaged 74.2 percent on this measure, substantially higher than low-scoring countries (62.0 percent). This factor is to some extent influenced by wealth, however, and after adjustment for economic conditions, it drops considerably in importance.

13. *Policy of investing in a large school library.* Countries vary considerably in the extent to which they make provision for school libraries. In DENMARK, SINGAPORE, the UNITED STATES, CANADA (BC), and SLOVENIA, principals report that their nine-year-olds have access to school libraries with over 7000 books, on average. By contrast, typical school libraries in PORTUGAL, INDONESIA, GERMANY (E), GREECE, TRINIDAD AND TOBAGO and the NETHER-

LANDS have fewer than 700 books. This study suggests that it is an important variable in accounting for differences in reading literacy levels. When book numbers were categorized by thousands, the high-scoring countries were found to have much larger school libraries, and the difference was even greater after adjustment for economic and social conditions.

14. *Policy of having large classroom libraries.* Some countries encourage schools to invest heavily in classroom "book-corners", where pupils can get more frequent access to books. The percentage of teachers reporting that they had a classroom library, and that it contained more than 60 books was determined. This figure revealed substantial differences in policy. In HONG KONG, CANADA (BC), the UNITED STATES and SINGAPORE, over 70 percent of students were in classrooms with large classroom libraries; in GERMANY (E), HUNGARY, and SLOVENIA, less than a third of teachers did. Table 5.3 indicates that this is one of the most important differential policies between high-scoring and low-scoring countries of all those examined and Table 5.4 confirms that it is not merely a sign of affluence. Effective reading programs are usually supported by large classroom libraries.

15. *Number of textbooks per student.* Research in developing countries has frequently given support for the provision of more textbooks as a key variable in raising achievement levels (e.g., Fuller 1987)). In this study, teachers were asked to estimate the number of textbooks available per student, but the question presented some difficulties at the nine-year-old level, as many countries make greater use of a range of children's books and other resources, rather than 'official' textbooks. The straight comparison of high and low-scoring countries did show a difference favoring more texts. Low provision was found in VENEZUELA, INDONESIA and TRINIDAD AND TOBAGO. However, this factor could be a function only of wealth in this study as it disappeared after adjustment for economic and social conditions. It could also be seen as a threshold variable, important only up to a particular level of provision. Further study is needed of this indicator, within countries.

16. *Frequency of book-borrowing by students.* It is one thing to provide books, but a more crucial question is whether students take advantage of this provision. Students were asked to report how often they borrowed books from school or public libraries, on a scale from *Never* (0) to *More than once a week* (5). While this variable may be suspect on reliability because of the doubtful ability of nine-year-olds to answer truthfully, it certainly showed a trend in the predictable direction. In high-scoring countries, students' borrowing mean was 3.27 (between *Once a week* and *Once a month*), while low-scorers averaged only 2.84. This observed difference was diminished after adjustment (see Table 5.4) but cannot be ignored. It merits further study.

17. *Time spent on teaching the language.* Countries vary in the amount of time assigned to teaching reading and related language activities in the weekly timetable. In NEW ZEALAND, the UNITED STATES, CANADA (BC), TRINIDAD AND TOBAGO and ITALY, teachers report spending 10 or more hours per week on language study; SLOVENIA and FINLAND report an average of only 3.9 hours, while GERMANY (W) (5.0), DENMARK (5.3), and INDONESIA (5.1) also give it low priority. A straight contrast shows that high-scoring countries do spend more time on language study and the difference is still clear-cut after adjusting for economic conditions. How that time is spent is no doubt critical, but cannot be explored at this stage.

18. *Frequency of silent reading by students in class.* In some countries, policies of independent silent reading in school are widely encouraged. In others, such a practice is not regarded as a valuable use of school time. Teachers were found to differ substantially between countries on this factor so it was analyzed further. In NEW ZEALAND, CANADA (BC) and HUNGARY, teachers reported this practice almost every day; in BELGIUM, DENMARK and INDONESIA, it was done less than once per week. In a straight contrast between high- and low-scoring countries there was no difference, but it was clearly an important factor in explaining differences between countries which fall above and below expectation on the basis of the CDI. Time spent reading in class is apparently not wasted time.

19. *Time spent by teachers reading aloud to pupils.* In some countries, teachers report that they spend much time reading to students in class. In CANADA (BC), NEW ZEALAND, PORTUGAL and GREECE, it occurs more than four times per week. By contrast, pupils in FRANCE rarely have this experience, while in HONG KONG, GERMANY (W), HUNGARY, INDONESIA and TRINIDAD AND TOBAGO, it happens less than one and a half times a week. In a straight comparison between high- and low-scoring countries, the difference favoring regular story reading is substantial. When adjusted for economic and social conditions, however, it is reduced to 0.25.

20. *Frequency of formal tests.* The teachers in the survey were asked to state how often they tested their students' reading formally. For each country the percentages of those who responded *weekly* or *monthly* were combined, and comparisons made between high and low scoring nations. While the first comparison showed a benefit for those who tested least often, this pattern was reversed when the results were corrected by the CDI measure. In the highest ten countries, after adjustment, 54 percent of teachers tested their children at least monthly; in the lowest achieving countries, only 32 percent did. This difference is a strong one, though not consistent in every case. Teachers in NEW ZEALAND, the UNITED STATES, and HUNGARY achieved high average scores without frequent testing. However, the relatively low figures of 3 percent, 5 percent, 8 percent, and 14 percent reported by teachers in DENMARK, NORWAY, GERMANY (W) and the NETHERLANDS respec-

tively, provide one probable reason for their scores, which were lower than expected.

21. *Students' speed of word recognition.* Although this is not a policy indicator, it is a likely influence on reading achievement. Most reading specialists see an important role for rapid word recognition in the reading process (Calfee and Drum 1986). The 40 item word-picture matching exercise given to Population A students was designed primarily to assess rapid word recognition, and thus to help explain low scores in the other domains. While the task is admittedly only an indirect measure of the recognition process, it is unlikely that poor decoders would perform well on it. As predicted, the ten high-scoring countries showed much higher average scores than the low-scoring nations, and the difference was still considerable after adjustment for CDI. In fact, the correlation between the national total achievement means and the percentage of students scoring below 50 percent on the word recognition test was 0.86. Furthermore, the gender differences on this test mirrored those of the other domains. Highest scoring countries in the Word Recognition Test were SINGAPORE, FINLAND, ITALY, the UNITED STATES and GREECE. Children in VENEZUELA, INDONESIA, DENMARK and GERMANY (E) produced unusually low average scores, which may help account for their lower achievement levels in the three other domains. It was noticeable that a few countries showed high performance levels in the Word Recognition Test without corresponding achievement in their Total Achievement scores, but that no country had the reverse pattern. Such patterns are consistent with the belief that rapid decoding is a prerequisite for good reading comprehension.

Educational Policy Indicators: Population B

Which educational policy variables are related to national achievement among 14-year-olds? Are the trends similar to those for Population A? A comparison of high- and low-scoring countries, before and after adjustment for economic and social differences, is again revealing.

Table 5.6 lists those factors which are associated with the largest differences between the ten highest and ten lowest scoring countries. Again, the figures were drawn from the National Case Study Questionnaire, and the other questionnaires completed by students, teachers and school principals. As some of the variables examined may well be regarded merely as correlates of wealth rather than of sound educational policy, a second table is given (Table 5.7) showing the contrast between the ten countries which showed higher average scores than were predicted by their economic and social status, and the ten countries which fell furthest below expectation. Any factor which clearly differentiates countries in both these contrasts must be considered an important variable, worthy of attention by policymakers and researchers.

Table 5.6. Relative importance of selected national policy indicators in relation to national achievement means for Population B.

Policy indicator	Highest 10 countries	Lowest 10 countries	Diff / SD	Difference as proportion of SD	Advantage for . . .
1 Average Class size	24.21	34.89	10.68/7.87	1.36	Smaller classes
2 Pupil-teacher ratio in school	0.065	0.048	0.017/0.023	0.74	More teachers per pupil
3 Average School size	631.8	936.0	304.2/402.6	0.76	Smaller schools
4 % Female teachers	65.7	68.5	2.80/18.69	0.15	No difference
5 School days per year	179.0	184.8	5.8/12.5	0.46	Shorter school year
6 Hours instruction per week	24.44	26.11	1.67/3.26	0.51	Shorter school hours
7 Years teacher education	15.27	14.26	1.01/1.90	0.53	More education for teachers
8 % Other language speaking teachers	10.6	38.1	28.5/28.9	0.99	More same language teachers
9 Frequency principal evaluates teachers	2.89	3.53	0.64/0.55	1.16	Less evaluation
10 Frequency students given homework	4.06	3.75	0.31/0.48	0.65	More general homework
11 Frequency students given rdg. homework	1.20	2.03	0.83/0.60	1.38	Less reading homework
12 Textbooks per student	1.69	1.10	0.59/0.51	1.16	More textbooks
13 Size of school library	5.20	2.50	2.70/2.84	0.95	More books
14 Level of resources for reading	4.05	3.14	0.91/1.11	0.82	More resources
15 Frequency of comprehension tests	.093	2.06	1.13/0.82	1.38	Fewer tests
16 Policy of individual tuition	62.1	41.9	20.2/26.5	0.76	More individual tuition

Table 5.7. Relative importance of selected national policy indicators for Population B after adjustment for economic and social conditions.

Policy indicator	Highest 10 countries	Lowest 10 countries	Diff / SD	Difference as proportion of SD	Advantage for . . .
1 Average Class size	26.48	27.32	0.84/7.87	0.11	No difference
2 Pupil-teacher ratio in school	0.065	0.064	0.001/0.023	0.04	No difference
3 Average School size	769.0	582.2	186.8/402.6	0.46	Larger schools
4 % Female teachers	76.40	51.10	25.30/18.69	1.35	More female teachers
5 School days per year	170.8	185.2	14.4/12.5	1.15	Shorter school year
6 Hours instruction per week	25.30	25.57	0.27/3.26	0.08	No difference
7 Years teacher education	15.60	14.72	0.88/1.40	0.63	More teacher education
8 % Other language speaking teachers	8.9	26.5	17.6/28.9	0.61	More official language speaking teachers
9 Frequency principal evaluates teachers	2.99	3.05	0.06/0.55	0.11	No difference
10 Frequency students given homework	4.16	3.73	0.43/0.48	0.90	More homework in general
11 Frequency students given rdg. homework	1.58	1.41	0.17/0.60	0.28	No difference
12 Textbooks per student	1.32	1.51	0.19/0.51	0.37	Fewer textbooks
13 Size of school library	4.20	2.70	1.50/2.84	0.53	Larger school libraries
14 Level of resources for reading	3.84	2.98	0.86/1.11	0.77	More resources
15 Frequency of comprehension tests	1.46	1.31	0.15/0.82	0.18	No difference
16 Policy of individual tuition	52.5	44.5	11.0/26.5	0.42	More individual tuition

It should be noted that the 31 countries which participated in the 14-year-old survey were not identical to the 27 which were involved in the 9-year-old survey. A few differences in the findings may then be attributable to the fact that the Population B study contained a larger number of developing countries.

1. *Average class size.* Countries whose teachers reported smaller classes certainly achieved better results at age 14 years. While the high-scoring countries have typical classes of 25, the low scorers have average class sizes nearer 35. This is one of the largest correlates of differences in literacy achievement. However, it is clearly a factor which is influenced by the ability to afford more teachers, and when adjusted for discrepancies in wealth the difference disappears.

2. *Pupil-teacher ratio in a school.* School principals also reported the number of pupils in their schools and the total number of teaching staff, excluding administrators and counselors. The pupil-teacher ratio, calculated from these figures, showed similar trends to those of the class-size variable. Countries with more favorable ratios obtained better results, but the differences virtually disappeared after CDI adjustment.

3. *Size of school.* Five countries reported average school enrollment figures over 1000 students, with particularly high numbers in the PHILIPPINES (1833), PORTUGAL (1565) and THAILAND (1691). By contrast, FINLAND, GREECE, ITALY, NORWAY, and SWITZERLAND reported schools of less than 400 students. A straightforward comparison of high- and low-scoring countries gives the advantage to countries with smaller schools (632 vs. 936 students), but this is again a policy associated with wealthier countries. When other things are made equal, countries with larger schools produce better results in relation to the resources they have available. Once again, these results are unduly influenced by two Asian countries, HONG KONG and SINGAPORE , with very large schools.

4. *Percentage of female teachers.* As in Population A, countries with larger proportions of female teachers show higher literacy achievement levels relative to their economic conditions. Before the adjustment there was little difference.

5. *Number of days per year the schools are open.* Once again, the advantage lies with countries which require students to attend school for less than 180 days per annum, before and after adjustment for resources. A shorter school year (within limits) does not appear to handicap students when judged on a criterion of reading literacy.

6. *Number of hours of instruction per week.* At age 14, countries which spend less time in school produce somewhat higher average achievement, but the difference may well be a function of wealth, and appears to be of little consequence after adjusting for level of development.

7. *Number of years of education for teachers.* As in Population A, a few countries expect their teachers to undergo long periods of education and training. CANADA (BC), GERMANY (W), ITALY, NORWAY, the UNITED STATES, and VENEZUELA all require more than 17 years; BOTSWANA, DENMARK, the NETHERLANDS, the PHILIPPINES, SINGAPORE, THAILAND and ZIMBABWE expect only 13 years or less. The extra years of education do suggest a positive influence, before and after adjustment for economic differences.

8. *Percentage of teachers whose first language is different from that of the school.* Countries which employ large numbers of teachers whose native language is different from that of the school do not produce as high literacy achievement levels in their students as native language speaking teachers, regardless of economic conditions in the country. This variable is more important at secondary school level than it proved to be with nine-year-olds.

9. *Frequency with which the school principal evaluates the work of teachers.* Policies concerning the role of the principal in evaluating teachers' work appear to vary considerably cross-culturally. This practice does not seem to have an influence on student reading achievement, however. In BOTSWANA, CYPRUS, ITALY, NIGERIA, the PHILIPPINES, and ZIMBABWE principals typically evaluate more than once per year, while in nine of the ten high-scoring countries teacher evaluations by the principal occur about once a year. The question is not relevant in SWITZERLAND's schools, which operate without full-time principals. In GREECE, PORTUGAL, DENMARK, and the NETHERLANDS, all middle-scoring countries, the practice is rarely undertaken. This variable warrants further investigation.

10. Frequency with which teachers assign general homework. In their comparative studies of Asian and American classrooms, Lee, Stigler and Stevenson (1988) identified amount of homework as one factor which enhances the performance levels of Asian students. They are expected to do more homework than American students, and it appeared to produce higher achievement. In this study there were also clear differences between high- and low-scoring countries favoring the value of general homework at the 14-year-old level. This pattern was repeated after adjusting for economic conditions. The amount of homework assigned appears to be a stable influence for reading literacy achievement across countries.

11. *Frequency with which teachers assign reading homework.* Apparently not all forms of homework are equally effective. Countries where teachers assigned large amounts of reading homework did not produce the same levels of achievement as those who assigned less. However, this difference disappeared after CDI adjustment, and is probably not conclusive. Cross-cultural differences in what teachers perceive as reading homework may have affected the outcome.

12. *Number of textbooks per student.* At the 9-year-old level, this factor showed a correlation with performance, but appeared to be more a sign of affluence than a cause of achievement. The same trend appeared at age fourteen. High-scoring countries did report more textbooks per student, but countries which achieved well above prediction had no more textbooks than those scoring below.

13. *Size of the school library.* As in the Population A survey, school library size is a powerful factor, differentiating clearly between high- and low-scoring countries, regardless of economic conditions. The top ten countries have libraries over twice as large as in the low-scoring countries, and the difference is almost as impressive after adjusting for CDI.

14. *Level of resources for reading.* School principals were asked to indicate whether their schools contained a set of eight facilities which were hypothesized to be indirect indicators of policies designed to encourage reading growth. The facilities were: a library, student reading room, student newspaper, teacher library, drama club, debating club, literature club and writing club. Highest on this combined indicator were SLOVENIA, SINGAPORE, NEW ZEALAND, the UNITED STATES, and HONG KONG, all close to an average of five resources; lowest were BOTSWANA, GERMANY (E), GREECE and VENEZUELA with less than two. Predictably, the high-scoring countries provided considerably more of these resources for encouraging reading, and the difference was even greater after adjusting for economic differences. These resources are either causes of or signs of commitment to higher literacy levels.

15. *Frequency with which teachers set comprehension tests of reading.* At the nine-year-old level more testing was related to higher achievement in the countries which scored above expectation, but this trend was not observed at the fourteen-year-old level. Teachers in the high-scoring countries reported less than half the frequency of testing than those in the lower achieving countries. Thus, FINLAND, NEW ZEALAND, SWEDEN and SWITZER-LAND produced high literacy levels with testing policies of less than once per week; by contrast, several other countries reported giving children reading comprehension tests three to four times a week, without apparent benefit. After adjustment for economic and social conditions, there was no difference on this variable.

16. *Provision of special individual tuition for students.* This policy varies widely across countries, and is therefore worthy of attention at this point. In DENMARK, HUNGARY, and ICELAND, over 90 percent of principals report such a policy; in FRANCE, GREECE, HONG KONG, and the NETHERLANDS, less than 20 percent reported it. The contrast between high- and low-scoring countries showed that it was a correlate of successful instruction, and after adjustment for CDI, it still appeared to be a favorable indicator.

Many other variables hypothesized to be correlated with achievement were captured in the questionnaires, and they will be investigated in further analyses, within and between countries.

Table 5.8. Summary of findings on policy indicators showing the comparisons unadjusted and adjusted for CDI: Populations A and B.

Advantage shown for:	Population A		Population B	
	Unadjusted	Adjusted for CDI	Unadjusted	Adjusted for CDI
1. Smaller classes	---	no	yes	---
2. More female teachers	---	yes	no	---
3. Shorter school year	yes	yes	yes	yes
4. More hours per week	yes	yes	no	---
5. More years teacher education	yes	yes	yes	yes
6. More textbooks per student	yes	---	yes	no
7. Larger school library	yes	yes	yes	yes
8. More formal tests	no	yes	no	---
9. Earlier starting age	no	yes		
10. High preschool enrollment	yes	---		
11. More multigrade classes	---	---		
12. More years with same class	---	no		
13. More books in community	yes	---		
14. Larger classroom library	yes	yes		
15. More library books borrowed	yes	yes		
16. More time teaching language	yes	yes		
17. More silent reading in class	---	yes		
18. More teacher reading to class	---	yes		
19. Students faster word recognition	yes	yes		
20. Better pupil-teacher ratio			yes	---
21. Principal evaluates teachers more often			no	---
22. More general homework given			yes	yes
23. More reading homework given			no	---
24. More resources for reading			yes	yes
25. More individual tuition			yes	yes

To assist the reader, a summary of the major findings from Tables 6.3, 6.4, 6.6 and 6.7 is presented in Table 5.8. This table lists, first, the policy variables which were analyzed in both populations, then those which were confined to only one population. The table shows in which cases each variable differentiated clearly between those countries in the high achievement levels and those with low achievement. A *Yes* in the adjoining column(s) denotes an advantage above 0.3 SD was found for the variable; a *No* denotes a disadvantage greater than 0.3 SD. A dash indicates that the correlation for that variable was less than 0.3. The table also shows whether the variable was still an important differentiating factor when the economic and social conditions of the country were adjusted for by the CDI.

Thus, in the case of Variable 1, an advantage was shown for *smaller classes* in a straight comparison of high and low achieving countries at both ages (columns 1 and 3). In Population A, however, the ten countries which achieved most above expectation had larger classes (column 2); in Population B there was no difference between countries which exceeded expectation and those which fall below expectation (column 4). A study of this table shows that some policy variables differentiate clearly at both levels in both kinds of analyses. The most prominent are *a shorter school year, more teacher education* and *larger school libraries*. For policy variables examined at Population A level only, the most consistent factors were *large classroom library, more books borrowed, more hours teaching the language, more silent reading* and *faster word recognition*. For variables unique to Population B, the consistent factor were *more general homework, more resources for reading* and *more individual tuition*.

The Case of FINLAND

It is clear that the students of FINLAND show consistently high average scores at both age levels across all kinds of reading. The question arises as to why their students are so successful. A full explanation of this question is beyond the scope of this booklet. There are no doubt many reasons, and some will be difficult to determine. They may lie, for instance, in the quality of the teaching and the value attached to literacy in the community. Nevertheless, a few tentative explanations can be offered, on the basis of information available at this stage.

1. *The Finnish language has an unusually regular orthography.* By and large each sound is represented by a single symbol, and each symbol stands for only one sound (Kyöstiö 1980). Many educators believe that this feature makes it easier for young children to crack the literacy code. While the benefits of such regularity are not apparent in this study across the whole range of languages, this factor cannot be ruled out for a language which is so nearly perfect in its phonetic correspondence. Certainly it is easier to justify a strong synthetic-phonic approach to literacy acquisition than in

other languages. Such methods are in common use, but teachers also report a variety of methods and emphasize comprehension, interest and critical thinking.

2. *FINLAND is a relatively wealthy country.* It has one of the highest GNPs per capita, and it spends more than most countries on its schools. Thus, it can attract able young people into teaching and afford smaller classes. The World Education Report (Unesco 1991) lists FINLAND as having the second best pupil-teacher ratio among the countries in this study. Health indicators are also impressive.

3. *The Finnish speaking schools are homogeneous linguistically.* FINLAND is a bilingual state where the 94% of the people speak Finnish and 5.8% speak Swedish as their native tongue. However, the Finnish and Swedish speaking children go to separate school systems from kindergarten to university. Only the Finnish speaking school system (95% of the students) participated in the international study, although the Swedish speaking system was assessed as a national option. Minority language students were not excluded from the testing if they attended Finnish speaking schools. However, the Finnish speaking classrooms are very homogeneous linguistically. Monolingual countries tend to have higher reading scores.

4. *Literacy is important in FINLAND.* It reports 99 percent adult literacy rate, the largest number of public library books per head in the sample, and one of the highest figures for newspaper circulation and book publication. Thus, there are probably many good adult models and high expectations exerted on children to learn to read.

Several other hypothetical reasons for the Finnish performance levels can be rejected at this stage.

1. *Early start:* Fewer than half the children can read at age seven when they enter school.

2. *More hours instruction in reading:* The Finnish timetable allows less than average time on reading, on language study and in school as a whole. However, the guiding phrase "Every teacher is a mother tongue teacher" is common in teacher training as well as in the written curriculum, especially in the primary level where an integrated curriculum has become the usual practice.

3. *More testing:* The number of teachers reporting frequent testing is only average, since testing in reading is not generally favored. Instead, Finnish teachers prefer student centered assessment methods that are closely designed for instruction, such as writing assignments, discussions, or project work. Some studies (e.g., Hiebert and Calfee 1992) support this type of assessment as correlated with high level performance.

4. *More teacher training:* The figures are again only average, and below average for in-service training. These numbers, however, reflect an over-lapping of two generations of teachers. Before 1977, primary teachers needed only three years of training and many of these teachers are still in the school system. Since 1977, teachers at all levels pursue academic studies for four to six years to complete the master's degree. The first teachers trained under the new system appeared in the schools in 1981. It should be noted that the teaching profession attracts candidates from among the most talented students in the high schools, especially girls.
5. *Less TV:* Finnish students watch TV just as much as their counterparts in other countries. It may be significant, however, that the children of FINLAND are exposed to many foreign TV films with Finnish subtitles which they have to read rapidly and often during the program (see Chapter 7).

This discussion has presented only a few of the possible factors at work in the Finnish culture and its educational policies which promote good reading among their young students. Several strong points, however, are clearly the result of thoughtful self-examination and planning within the profession and warrant further investigation.

CHAPTER SIX

DIFFERENCES IN ACHIEVEMENT BY GENDER, HOME LANGUAGE AND URBAN-RURAL LOCATION

Gender Differences

Previous international studies of reading have shown that girls tend to surpass boys in most countries and cultures, both in their reading interest (Guthrie and Greaney 1991) and their achievement levels in reading (Thorndike 1973, Downing 1972). Opinion differs however, as to whether these differences are primarily maturational or culturally conditioned. Preston (1962) found empirical support for the latter view when he showed that boys surpassed girls in reading achievement in GERMANY, but were consistently behind girls in the UNITED STATES. He noted that, at that time, male teachers predominated in primary schools in Germany, while the reverse was true in American schools. Building on this research, Johnson (1974) investigated gender difference in reading at Grades 2, 4 and 6 in four countries, and found support for Preston's position. Boys in NIGERIA and GERMANY achieved well and more often had been taught by male teachers than boys in CANADA and the UNITED STATES where the boys fared less well than the girls. A plausible explanation is that boys identify better with the values of male teachers than with female teachers.

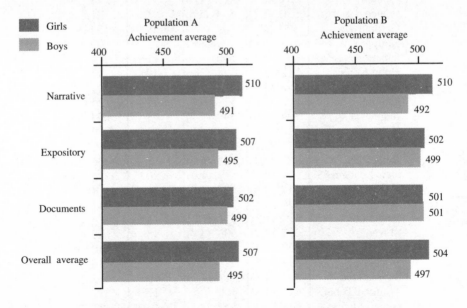

Figure 6.1. Differences in reading achievement of boys and girls across all countries by domain and overall, favoring girls

In the present study, gender comparisons were made across all countries at both age levels and further light was thrown on this issue. Tables 6.1 and 6.2 present the score differences in raw form and in standard score form. In the column marked 'difference' an asterisk is placed next to those values where, after taking into account the standard errors of sampling, the differences are significant. For Population A the following results were found:

1. Girls achieved at higher levels in all countries. There was no country where boys were ahead in the overall score (Figure 6.1). Girls were also consistently ahead in Narrative and Expository reading.
2. The smallest differences were found in the Documents domain in every case. In fact, the boys' average scores actually exceeded the girls' slightly in six countries: FRANCE, GERMANY (W), the NETHERLANDS, SWITZERLAND, SPAIN, and the UNITED STATES.

Table 6.1. Gender differences in overall scores (with standard error of sampling) by country: Population A

Country	Average score (s.e.)		Difference	Standard score difference
	Boys	Girls		
Belgium/Fr	503 (4.5)	512 (4.5)	9	.12
Canada/BC	495 (5.4)	506 (5.4)	11*	.14
Cyprus	479 (3.2)	484 (3.2)	5	.07
Denmark	463 (5.5)	489 (4.9)	26*	.34
Finland	564 (4.5)	575 (4.5)	11*	.14
France	530 (5.7)	533 (5.6)	3	.04
Germany/E	490 (6.3)	509 (6.1)	19*	.24
Germany/W	501 (3.9)	508 (3.8)	7	.09
Greece	499 (4.4)	510 (4.2)	11*	.14
Hong Kong	512 (3.7)	524 (3.6)	12*	.15
Hungary	495 (3.8)	504 (3.6)	9	.11
Iceland	508 (0.0)	528 (0.0)	20*	.24
Indonesia	394 (3.6)	397 (3.7)	3	.04
Ireland	502 (5.2)	517 (5.0)	15*	.19
Italy	525 (5.2)	537 (5.1)	12*	.15
Netherlands	483 (5.4)	488 (5.2)	5	.06
New Zealand	519 (4.1)	539 (4.0)	20*	.25
Norway	517 (4.6)	533 (4.0)	16*	.18
Portugal	474 (4.5)	483 (4.5)	9	.11
Singapore	510 (1.3)	521 (1.3)	11*	.14
Slovenia	491 (3.3)	506 (3.4)	15*	.19
Spain	500 (3.4)	508 (3.3)	8*	.10
Sweden	533 (4.4)	546 (4.3)	13*	.16
Switzerland	507 (4.2)	517 (4.2)	10*	.13
Trinidad/Tobago	443 (4.3)	460 (4.1)	17*	.21
United States	543 (3.6)	552 (3.4)	9*	.11
Venezuela	379 (4.2)	392 (3.9)	13*	.16

* = significant difference (.05 level)

3. The largest differences between boys and girls were found in the Narrative domain, in almost every case. In six countries, DENMARK, NEW ZEALAND, ICELAND, GERMANY (E), NORWAY and TRINIDAD AND TOBAGO, the differences were quite considerable.

These gender differences are not very large. There are very good male readers in every country, and many boys achieve well above the average girl in every country. However, in 17 of the 27 countries at the Population A level the girls' mean was greater by at least ten points on the average score. The very consistency of this gender gap across cultures at age nine provides some support for a maturational viewpoint.

Table 6.2. Gender differences in overall scores (with standard error of sampling) by country: Population B

Country	Average score (s.e.)		Difference	Standard score difference
	Boys	Girls		
Belgium/Fr	480 (5.2)	486 (5.4)	6	.08
Botswana	327 (3.2)	333 (2.8)	6	.08
Canada/BC	513 (3.4)	534 (3.3)	21*	.29
Cyprus	493 (3.0)	501 (3.2)	8*	.11
Denmark	523 (2.9)	527 (2.8)	4	.06
Finland	554 (3.7)	568 (3.6)	14*	.19
France	553 (5.0)	549 (4.2)	-4	-.06
Germany/E	523 (4.0)	530 (4.0)	7	.10
Germany/W	522 (4.4)	526 (4.4)	4	.06
Greece	509 (3.3)	510 (3.1)	1	.01
Hong Kong	533 (4.0)	538 (3.8)	5	.07
Hungary	528 (3.8)	542 (3.7)	14*	.19
Iceland	530 (0.0)	543 (0.0)	13*	.18
Ireland	502 (5.1)	525 (5.0)	23*	.28
Italy	511 (4.0)	520 (3.9)	9*	.13
Netherlands	511 (4.9)	520 (5.2)	9	.11
New Zealand	544 (5.9)	549 (5.5)	5	.07
Nigeria	401 (----)	401 (----)	0	-.01
Norway	516 (3.2)	520 (3.1)	4	.06
Philippines	427 (3.4)	432 (2.6)	5	.07
Portugal	528 (3.4)	520 (3.2)	-8*	-.11
Singapore	534 (1.6)	534 (1.5)	0	-.01
Slovenia	529 (3.3)	534 (3.3)	5	.07
Spain	488 (3.3)	492 (3.1)	4	.06
Sweden	540 (3.3)	555 (3.2)	15*	.21
Switzerland	535 (3.5)	538 (3.3)	3	.04
Thailand	464 (7.3)	488 (5.5)	24*	.33
Trinidad/Tobago	466 (2.6)	492 (2.2)	26*	.36
United States	530 (6.3)	543 (5.9)	13*	.18
Venezuela	419 (4.0)	421 (3.5)	2	.03
Zimbabwe	380 (4.4)	363 (4.1)	-17*	-.24

* = significant difference (.05 level)

However, the proportion of female teachers in the schools represented in the study did vary considerably, from 86 percent in SLOVENIA to 50 percent in INDONESIA. Thus it was possible to investigate further the hypothesis that boys' performance relative to girls' is reduced by the preponderance of female teachers in the primary school (Table 6.3).

Table 6.3. Percentage of female teachers in primary schools of countries with large and small discrepancies in gender means: Population A

	Country	Score discrepancy	% Female teachers
Large Gender Gaps	Denmark	26	57
	New Zealand	20	82
	Germany/East	19	75
	Iceland	20	68
	Trinidad/Tobago	17	73
	Mean	20.4	70.9
Small Gender Gaps	Indonesia	3	50
	France	3	67
	Netherlands	5	53
	Cyprus	5	55
	Germany/West	7	71
	Mean	4.6	59.2

In fact, there is some support for the teacher gender position in these figures. In the five countries where 9-year-old girls were found to be furthest ahead of boys, 71 percent of the primary school teachers were female; in the countries with the smallest gender gap, there were only 59 percent. It should be noted, however, that DENMARK, with the biggest gap, had 57 percent female teachers while FRANCE, with the second smallest gap, had 67 percent female teachers. There are clearly other factors at work here.

Another hypothesis emerges from these findings, however. Three of the six countries with the largest gender gap start reading instruction at age five – NEW ZEALAND, TRINIDAD AND TOBAGO and IRELAND – and in two of these countries, the boys are furthest behind at age fourteen. As a starting age of five is found in only four countries, it is clearly a plausible hypothesis that boys are too immature to begin reading formally at age five, and that their difficulties are represented in low achievement, relative to girls, at both age levels.

Table 6.2 presents the gender differences in overall achievement for Population B. At this level the gender gap has clearly narrowed in all but nine countries. In fact, the mean difference dropped from 11.6 points to 7.1 points overall, and in two countries, ZIMBABWE and PORTUGAL, the boys showed significantly higher means in average scores. Nevertheless, it is still the case, world-wide, that girls are better readers at age fourteen, particularly in the Narrative domain. Whatever cultural factors operated to produce better female readers at age nine were exerting even stronger effects at age 14 in TRINIDAD AND TOBAGO, IRELAND and CANADA (BC). However, the boys showed a marked improvement in DENMARK, NEW ZEALAND, GERMANY (E), SLOVENIA, GREECE, NORWAY, PORTUGAL, SINGAPORE and VENEZUELA. All gained ten points or more on the girls' achievement levels in these countries; the DANISH boys gained 22 points.

The reasons for these changing differences in gender gaps will be investigated further in other booklets in this series.

Home Language Differences

How many students receive schooling in a second language?
A perennial issue in linguistically diverse countries is the question of the language of instruction for acquiring literacy. Conventional wisdom has it that students whose home language is that of the school will have an easier transition into reading than those who have to learn a new language while they learn to read. Indeed, Unesco has repeatedly urged that children be taught to read in their home language where possible (Malmquist 1991). Although Wagner (1991) has argued a contrary position, researchers in bilingual education generally agree. Therefore, non-native speaking groups would be expected to score at lower levels on reading literacy tests which are presented in the official language.

To explore this matter, students were asked to state how often they used the *language of the test* at home. At the 9-year-old level, more than half of the students in two countries – SINGAPORE (73 percent) and INDONESIA (73 percent) – reported that they *never* or *hardly ever* spoke the school language at home. At the 14-year-old level, the countries with large numbers of such students were BOTSWANA (61 percent), PHILIPPINES (90 percent), SINGAPORE (74 percent) and ZIMBABWE (83 percent). Among the remaining countries NIGERIA, ITALY and THAILAND also had more than 20 percent different home language students.

Most European countries reported less than 15 percent of such children in their samples at the 9-year-old level, and these figures dropped off consistently at age fourteen. The most linguistically homogeneous populations were FIN-LAND, GERMANY (E), HUNGARY and IRELAND with three percent or less second language students at the Population A level.

How serious is a language discrepancy between home and school?
Tables 6.4 and 6.5 list, for both populations, the countries in order of the size of the achievement discrepancy between the average scores (combined across domains) for those learning in their home language and those who were not.

Table 6.4. Mean reading achievement score for students speaking a different
language at home and for students speaking the school language:
Population A

Country	Non-school language		School language		Home language achievement gap
	% of students in sample	Average score (s.e.)	% of students in sample	Average score (s.e.)	
New Zealand	8.4	465 (9.6)	91.6	535 (3.0)	70
Sweden	9.2	486 (10.8)	90.8	544 (3.2)	58
Norway	4.1	471 (16.7)	95.9	527 (3.1)	56
Germany/West	10.5	461 (8.1)	89.5	509 (2.9)	48
France	9.1	491 (12.2)	90.9	536 (4.2)	45
Switzerland	20.7	476 (6.3)	79.3	521 (3.2)	45
Denmark	4.7	441 (15.9)	95.3	480 (3.8)	39
Singapore	72.5	505 (1.1)	27.5	543 (1.9)	38
Finland	1.5	532 (27.6)	98.5	569 (3.2)	37
Greece	6.4	472 (12.6)	93.6	508 (3.1)	36
Hong Kong	12.6	488 (7.3)	87.4	522 (2.8)	34
Slovenia	11.5	469 (6.8)	88.5	502 (2.5)	33
Hungary	2.8	468 (14.3)	97.2	501 (2.7)	33
Iceland	3.5	487 (0.0)	96.5	519 (0.0)	32
Belgium/France	11.4	481 (9.5)	88.6	512 (3.3)	31
Netherlands	12.5	459 (11.0)	87.5	489 (4.0)	30
UnitedStates	3.5	520 (12.3)	96.5	549 (2.5)	29
Germany/East	1.7	472 (28.4)	98.3	500 (4.4)	28
Italy	26.9	513 (6.9)	73.1	537 (4.1)	24
Trinidad/Tobago	14.7	439 (7.9)	85.3	456 (3.2)	17
Ireland	3.0	495 (23.2)	97.0	510 (3.7)	15
Canada/BC	11.0	488 (10.4)	89.0	502 (4.1)	14
Portugal	3.4	469 (19.1)	96.6	479 (3.2)	10
Indonesia	72.5	394 (3.0)	27.5	403 (5.1)	9
Spain	13.4	499 (6.2)	86.6	505 (2.5)	6
Cyprus	3.7	476 (13.6)	96.3	482 (2.3)	6
Venezuela	17.8	383 (6.3)	82.2	388 (3.2)	5

At the top of this list of *home language achievement gaps*, at both age levels,
is NEW ZEALAND whose non-English speaking children scored 70 points below
the mainstream English-speaking students at the 9-year-old level, and 81 points
at age fourteen. The minorities in this case were made up predominantly of
Pacific Island students, whose literacy traditions are often not strong, although
they may value education highly. These students are clearly experiencing
difficulties with reading requirements in the official language.

For Population A, second language students in SWEDEN and NORWAY also
scored well below students who spoke the official language, by 58 and 56 points
respectively. By contrast, the non-native language speakers of CYPRUS, VENEZU-
ELA, SPAIN and INDONESIA were reading almost as well as the native speakers in
those countries.

Table 6.5. Mean reading achievement score for students speaking a different
language at home and for students speaking the school language:
Population B

| Country | Non-school language | | School language | | Home language achieve- ment gap |
	% of students in sample	Average score (s.e.)	% of students in sample	Average score (s.e.)	
New Zealand	5.6	470 (15.9)	94.4	551 (4.1)	81
Germany/West	8.4	455 (10.7)	91.6	530 (3.2)	75
United States	3.8	478 (21.0)	96.2	539 (4.4)	61
Cyprus	0.4	437 (32.1)	99.6	497 (2.2)	60
Denmark	2.5	470 (12.9)	97.5	527 (2.0)	57
Belgium/French	8.7	435 (13.3)	91.3	491 (3.9)	56
Sweden	5.1	501 (10.8)	94.9	549 (2.3)	48
Switzerland	15.0	497 (6.7)	85.0	544 (2.5)	47
Norway	1.9	473 (19.5)	98.1	519 (2.2)	46
Hungary	0.6	493 (35.9)	99.4	536 (2.7)	43
Singapore	74.1	523 (1.2)	25.9	566 (2.3)	43
Hong Kong	4.1	495 (14.9)	95.9	537 (2.8)	42
Italy	26.1	488 (5.1)	73.9	525 (3.3)	37
France	3.9	516 (16.1)	96.1	552 (3.3)	36
Ireland	1.2	482 (44.7)	98.8	513 (3.6)	31
Trinidad/Tobago	16.1	456 (3.9)	83.9	485 (1.9)	29
Finland	0.6	533 (38.1)	99.4	562 (2.6)	29
Netherlands	9.1	489 (12.6)	90.9	518 (3.7)	29
Iceland	0.4	508 (0.0)	99.6	536 (0.0)	28
Slovenia	6.3	506 (8.5)	93.7	534 (2.3)	28
Venezuela	5.3	394 (11.7)	94.7	421 (2.6)	27
Greece	2.8	487 (13.4)	97.2	510 (2.3)	23
Philippines	89.6	428 (2.1)	10.4	449 (8.1)	21
Portugal	1.6	504 (18.6)	98.4	524 (2.4)	20
Canada/BC	7.6	506 (8.3)	92.4	524 (2.4)	18
Zimbabwe	83.2	371 (3.1)	16.8	385 (9.3)	14
Spain	11.4	481 (6.8)	88.6	491 (2.4)	10
Botswana	61.4	328 (2.7)	38.6	334 (3.4)	6
Germany/East	0.8	521 (32.1)	99.2	527 (2.8)	6
Thailand	38.7	476 (6.8)	61.3	479 (6.0)	3
Nigeria	41.2	403 (*)	58.8	400 (*)	-3

* Insufficient data to calculate the Design Effect

For Population B, the largest discrepancies, after NEW ZEALAND (81), were
shown by GERMANY (W) (75), the UNITED STATES(61), CYPRUS (60), DENMARK
(57), BELGIUM (FR) (56). On the other hand, second language students appear to
have relatively less difficulty reading the school language in NIGERIA, THAILAND,
GERMANY (E), BOTSWANA and SPAIN.

How much are the national means affected by the presence of large numbers
of different home language students? The average scores for students who speak
the official language, as presented in Tables 6.4 and 6.5, are in most cases within

three to five points of the national averages for the total sample. For SINGAPORE 9-year-olds however, the 28 percent of students who claimed to speak English at least *often* in their home scored an average of 543 which is 28 points higher than the national mean, and close to the highest national means in the study. The 14-year-olds who spoke the test language (English) at home performed even better, with a mean of 566, which is the highest of all countries. As noted earlier, there are many students in SINGAPORE whose reading levels are well above expectation. Even those whose home language is not the test language showed scores above the international mean. Only FINLAND, the UNITED STATES and ITALY showed similar patterns in Population A.

At Population B level, those students not speaking the test language at home in GERMANY (E), FRANCE, and FINLAND all scored well above the international mean. It should be borne in mind that school systems with large numbers of students not speaking the test language at home are more likely to have special instruction for these students than schools with small numbers of them especially in Population A.

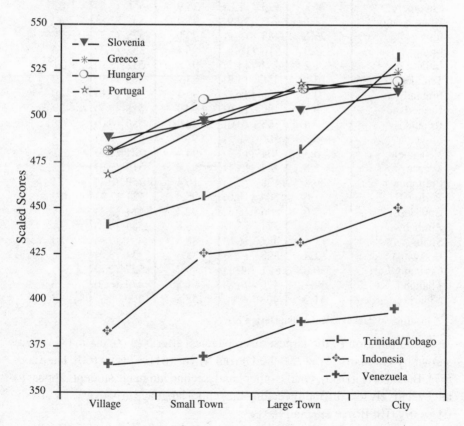

Figure 6.2. Mean scores for seven countries with largest advantage
for urban students, Population A

Urban-Rural Differences

Traditionally, urban students have had many educational advantages not enjoyed by their rural counterparts. Schools typically have better resources in the cities, better qualified teachers prefer to live in cities, and more cultural amenities are usually available for students. Such advantages have typically been reflected in higher achievement levels for urban children, especially at the secondary school level. In the present study this was the case in most countries. At the 9-year-old level, a group of seven countries, predominantly with lower national economic indicators, followed this pattern of lower performance levels in rural schools, and progressively higher scores as the size of the community increases (Figure 6.2). Students in cities are typically more proficient than the children from small villages by half a standard deviation. (The values for these figures are found in Appendix G.)

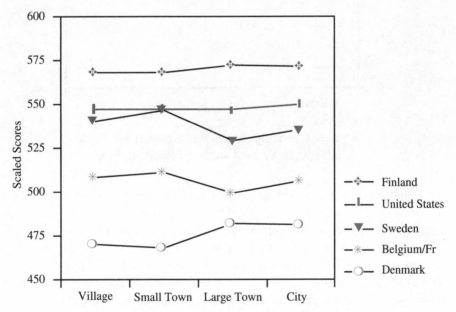

Figure 6.3. Average scores for countries with negligible differences
between urban and rural conditions: Population A

However, a number of countries have been able to narrow the gap in educational and cultural opportunities by providing rural library facilities, establishing teacher recruitment schemes to attract good teachers to rural schools, setting up better transport systems and other such measures. Such policies of equalizing amenities could well be reflected in the flat graph produced for Population A in five countries. FINLAND, SWEDEN, DENMARK, BELGIUM (FR) and the UNITED STATES show no gap at all between urban and rural students' achievement levels (Figure 6.3). An alternative interpretation, of course, is that the students in urban areas in these countries are disadvantaged due to poverty and depressed living conditions.

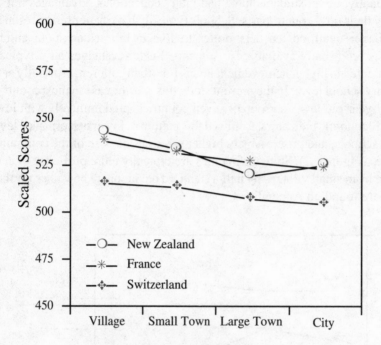

Figure 6.4. Average scores for three countries with
advantage for rural students: Population A

Finally, there is a group of three countries with an unusual pattern of scores favoring rural schools. In FRANCE, SWITZERLAND and NEW ZEALAND it is the urban students who are disadvantaged at age 9 (Figure 6.4). Only in NEW ZEALAND, however, was this rural advantage carried through to secondary school.

Despite these few unusual cases, this chapter has shown that there is a consistency in patterns of achievement across countries favoring girls, students who speak the language of the school, and students from urban areas.

CHAPTER SEVEN

OTHER INFLUENCES ON ACHIEVEMENT

Availability of Books

Surveys of achievement in a number of countries have shown that the numbers of books available to students is a key factor influencing their levels of reading ability (Fuller 1987). Furthermore, a recent review of "book flood" studies in six countries, in which large numbers of high interest books were provided for schools, showed consistently beneficial effects (Elley 1991). The findings reported in Chapter 5 about the mean size of school and class libraries are also consistent with these conclusions. It seems that good readers require a plentiful supply of books. As a variable which policymakers can influence, it is worthy of further study across all countries.

The present survey investigated the availability of books by asking students, teachers and school principals to estimate the numbers of books there were in the students' homes and at school, and the availability of libraries and book-stores in the students' neighborhoods.

Number of books at home

In both age groups, the number of books students reported at home showed clear-cut relationships with their achievement levels. Students were asked to estimate the number of books there were in their homes – from 0 to over 200 – in six categories.

At population B level, the median number of students reporting more than 100 books in the home was near 50 percent, with particularly high numbers in CANADA (BC), DENMARK, HUNGARY, ICELAND, NEW ZEALAND, NORWAY, SWEDEN. By contrast BOTSWANA, CYPRUS, GREECE, HONG KONG, the PHILIPPINES and ZIMBABWE, all reported less than 30 percent of homes with 100 or more books.

Similar patterns were found at the 9-year-old level. Countries vary considerably in the availability of books in the home and these differences are clearly reflected in national literacy levels.

More important for this survey is the pattern of achievement levels in relation to these figures. Figure 7.1 presents the scaled scores averaged over domains, for selected Population A countries for students who reported 0, 1-10, 11-50, 51-100, 101-200 and over 200 books respectively. The same information averaged over all countries is included for comparison. (The values for the figures in this chapter can be found in Appendix G.)

Figure 7.1 reveals a steady upward rise in achievement at least to 51-100 books, and up to 200 for four countries, with a leveling off for the majority of countries at that point. It is perhaps surprising that HONG KONG students managed to achieve at high levels without many books, along with the better resourced countries of FINLAND, FRANCE and the UNITED STATES. In no country did students achieve well from a background of bookless homes, and only in HONG KONG, FINLAND and the UNITED STATES did 9-year-olds score above the international mean of 500 when there were fewer than ten books at home. Clearly ready access to books at home seems to be an ingredient in making a good reader.

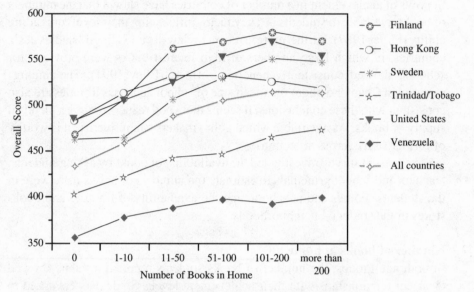

Figure 7.1. Average scores by number of books in home: Selected countries compared with all countries: Population A

An even stronger pattern was observed in Population B. In 21 countries there was a steady increase in achievement in relation to the size of family book holdings, up to 200 plus. The threshold number of books for better reading performance at this age is somewhat higher than for 9-year-olds.

Size of school library
The number of books in the school library is an indicator of the extent to which schools are prepared to encourage students to read. To investigate this relationship in each country, school principals were asked to estimate how many books their libraries contained. The data show considerable diversity between countries in average library size. Several developing countries, namely BOTSWANA, the PHILIPPINES, VENEZUELA and ZIMBABWE had predominantly small school libraries or none at all, while DENMARK, SINGAPORE, the UNITED STATES, CANADA (BC) and SLOVENIA typically had school libraries of more than 7,000 at both age levels. However, at the Population B level, schools in NEW ZEALAND, SWEDEN and THAILAND also have an average of more than 7,000 books.

As in previous surveys of individual countries, a clear link was found between reading ability and the size of school libraries. For each country the schools were grouped into quarters by size of school library. The overall scores for each quarter in each country were then computed and the means aggregated across all countries (492, 500, 504, 515). A regular increase in average score was observed with increases in library size across all countries and within most of them. In FINLAND, GERMANY (E) and ITALY the relationship was not so regular, but the data for all other countries are consistent with the proposition that a large stock of books is a prerequisite for an effective reading program. There is also an apparent difference between wealthier and poorer countries as defined by the CDI. Figure 7.2 illustrates this pattern for the top ten countries and the bottom ten countries on the CDI in relation to the pattern for all countries. Apparently a threshold of advantage is found in the high CDI school systems in the third quarter.

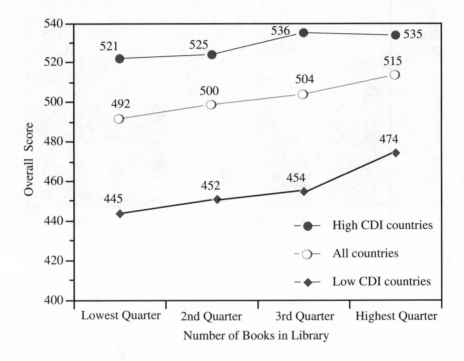

Figure 7.2. School library size by achievement: Population B

Availability of bookstores
Another aspect of children's accessibility to books is the availability of nearby bookstores. School principals were asked to indicate whether bookstores were available locally (within 30 minutes travel time), or nearby (in a neighboring town or city) or not available (within two hours traveling time). Only in the developing countries did substantial numbers of principals indicate that their students had the lowest access level (Figure 7.3), although most countries had

about 4 percent of such students. Just over 80 percent of 14-year-old students, overall, had easy access to book stores.

Furthermore, in 22 countries, the highest achievement was shown by 14-year-old students with easy access. By contrast, large numbers of students in the four lowest scoring countries had poor access. The average score for all these students was less than 380.

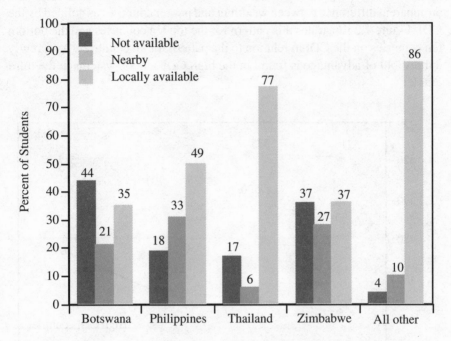

Figure 7.3. Access to bookstores in four developing countries and in all other countries: Population B

Self Ratings in Reading

How accurate are students' perceptions of their own ability in reading? Do these perceptions differ across countries? In this survey, students were asked to rate their ability on a four point scale: *Very Good*, *Good*, *Average* or *Not Very Good*.

Figure 7.4 presents for Population A the percentage of students in each country who rated their ability in each category with the countries arranged in order of overall achievement level. For easier interpretation, the right hand side of the figure shows a graph of the percentage of students in each country who rated their ability as *Good* or *Very Good*.

A study of this graph shows considerable variation in the ability of students to rate themselves internationally. FINLAND, FRANCE, HONG KONG and SINGAPORE show high percentages of students (more than 44 percent) who claim to be *Average* or *Not Very Good*, yet their overall achievement levels are very strong.

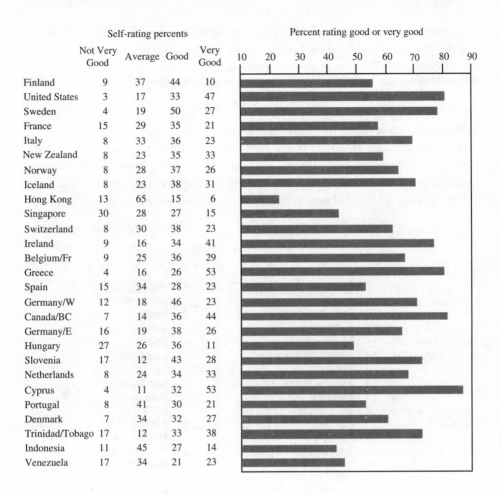

	Self-rating percents				Percent rating good or very good
	Not Very Good	Average	Good	Very Good	
Finland	9	37	44	10	
United States	3	17	33	47	
Sweden	4	19	50	27	
France	15	29	35	21	
Italy	8	33	36	23	
New Zealand	8	23	35	33	
Norway	8	28	37	26	
Iceland	8	23	38	31	
Hong Kong	13	65	15	6	
Singapore	30	28	27	15	
Switzerland	8	30	38	23	
Ireland	9	16	34	41	
Belgium/Fr	9	25	36	29	
Greece	4	16	26	53	
Spain	15	34	28	23	
Germany/W	12	18	46	23	
Canada/BC	7	14	36	44	
Germany/E	16	19	38	26	
Hungary	27	26	36	11	
Slovenia	17	12	43	28	
Netherlands	8	24	34	33	
Cyprus	4	11	32	53	
Portugal	8	41	30	21	
Denmark	7	34	32	27	
Trinidad/Tobago	17	12	33	38	
Indonesia	11	45	27	14	
Venezuela	17	34	21	23	

Figure 7.4. Self-ratings at each of four levels, listed by order
of national achievement level: Population A

More confident, on this scale, are the students of CYPRUS, GREECE, CANADA (BC)
and the UNITED STATES who rate themselves as *Very Good*. Only in the latter case
would this confidence seem to be well justified. Indeed, there was no relationship between the percentage of students in a country rating their reading ability
as *Very Good* and their national achievement level. This kind of discrepancy
between achievement and self-perception on an international scale has been
noted before (Lapointe et al. 1989) and clearly reflects cultural norms about
modesty.

Of course, it is a very difficult task for students to view their ability in an
international perspective. Within their own country there was in fact a much
higher relationship between their ratings and their actual achievement levels. In
most countries the correlations were between 0.25 and 0.55 with Narrative and
Expository scores, and slightly less for Document scores. Only in HONG KONG,

INDONESIA and VENEZUELA did students appear to have real difficulty in making assessments of this kind. In GERMANY (E), DENMARK, SWITZERLAND, SLOVENIA and GERMANY (W) they were very good at it.

TV Viewing

How much television do students watch?

As television and video are prime contenders for children's potential reading time, it is appropriate to examine trends in TV viewing hours. Students were asked to estimate how often they watched TV daily, choosing from five time categories. Figure 7.5 shows the percentage of students in both age groups who

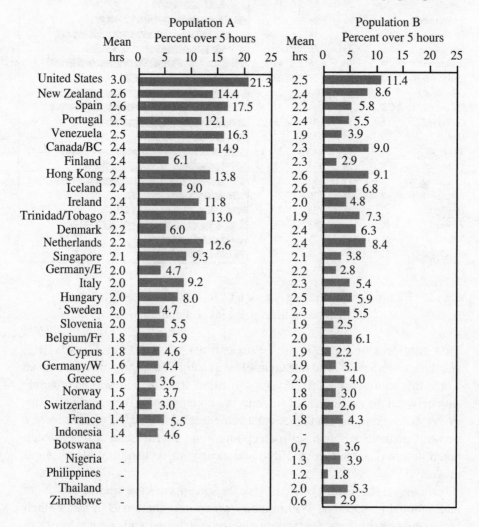

Figure 7.5. Mean hours daily TV viewing and percent of students reporting over five hours per day

claim to watch over five hours per day, together with the mean number of reported hours based on all levels of viewing. These figures are based on students' recollections which may sometimes be inaccurate, but the similarity of the statistics for the two age levels is high and suggests reasonable accuracy.

In Population A, the UNITED STATES stands out. American 9-year-olds claim to watch three hours of television per day, and some 21 percent watch for over five hours per day. Many children are spending considerably more time in front of their TV sets than they spend in school. Other heavy viewing countries, at this age, are NEW ZEALAND, and three Latin countries, SPAIN, PORTUGAL and VENEZU-ELA, all close to 2.5 hours, while children of CANADA (BC), ICELAND, FINLAND, HONG KONG and IRELAND report 2.4 hours per day.

By contrast, children of FRANCE, SWITZERLAND and INDONESIA watch only 1.4 hours per school day on average, and many in these countries watch none at all. Such patterns leave considerably more time for leisure reading, if that is the student's preference. At the 14-year-old level the mean viewing hours are very similar although fewer pupils claim to watch over five hours daily. Students in ICELAND, HONG KONG, HUNGARY and the UNITED STATES show the highest viewing rates, at 2.5 hours or more, while BOTSWANA and ZIMBABWE report an average of less than one hour daily.

How does TV viewing affect reading literacy scores?

How serious is it for their reading progress that students spend so much time in front of their TV screens? Could they be learning something there which pays off in their general reading? This is clearly not true for the majority, although further analysis may reveal exceptions. In most countries there was a negative relationship between reading achievement and level of viewing. Light viewers generally scored more highly.

The most clear-cut cases of a downward sloping curve for heavy TV viewing at age nine are found in the UNITED STATES, SWITZERLAND, BELGIUM, FRANCE and GERMANY (W), whose achievement patterns are plotted in Figure 7.6. In such countries, light viewers score highly, heavy viewers poorly. Whatever the viewing diet of these students is, it is apparently not beneficial to their reading.

Similar patterns were found for these five countries at the 14-year-old level, and DENMARK, NEW ZEALAND, and IRELAND also showed regular downward slopes at that age.

By contrast, there is a group of five countries in which moderately heavy viewing – up to three and a half hours daily – is associated with higher reading performance among 9-year-olds (Figure 7.7). Either these students have found ways of fitting both forms of activity into their lives, or the frequent TV viewing may actually contribute, indirectly, to better reading. In this respect there is a recently formulated hypothesis which gains support from the trends in Figure 7.7. Most of the students in the countries represented in this figure are regularly exposed to imported foreign language films on their television channels. These

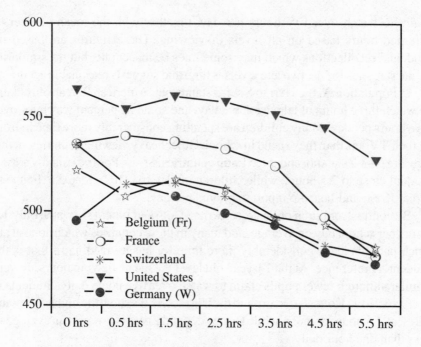

Figure 7.6. Pattern of decreasing reading achievement with
increasing TV viewing: Population A

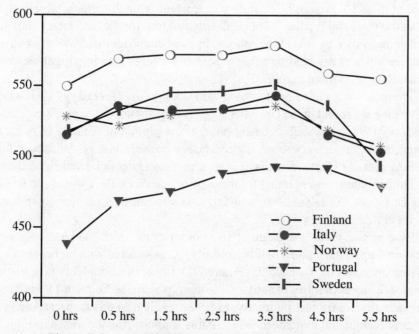

Figure 7.7. Pattern of increasing reading achievement with
moderately heavy TV viewing: Population A

films are often shown with sub-titles in the local language. There is, in fact, recent experimental evidence to show that this practice is beneficial for children's reading (Neuman and Kostinen 1992). Regular experiences of rapid reading under highly motivating circumstances, with pictorial cues to support meaning, is apparently a productive practice for raising reading levels in younger students. This practice clearly merits further investigation.

At the Population B level, the only countries to show an upward trend, favoring moderately heavy viewers, were the PHILIPPINES, PORTUGAL, SLOVENIA, VENEZUELA and ZIMBABWE. Most of these are countries where the actual presence of television may be an indicator of higher socio-economic status, so the figures could be misleading. In most countries, the downward trends confirm that heavy viewing is not readily compatible with high reading achievement at the 14-year-old level.

CHAPTER EIGHT

HOW DOES ONE BECOME
A GOOD READER?

Students at both age levels were asked to consider eleven different strategies which they might use if they wished to become a better reader, and to choose the three ways they believed were most important. The main purposes of this question were:

1. To provide some information about the kinds of literacy acquisition strategies which were promoted by the teachers in each country, as perceived by the pupils.
2. To reveal which strategies are most often associated with high achievement in each country.

Table 8.1 lists the eleven options from which the students chose, arranged in order of popularity for Population A. The percentages given for each population were calculated by averaging the percentages of students in each country who chose each option. All countries were given equal weight in this analysis.

Table 8.1. Percentages of students choosing each strategy for becoming a good reader: Populations A and B

Strategy choices	Percent students selecting strategy	
	Pop A	Pop B
Liking it.	58	69
Having lots of time to read.	37	33
Being able to concentrate well.	36	48
Knowing how to sound out words.	34	24
Learning the meaning of lots of words.	25	35
Having many good books around.	20	27
Lots of drill at the hard things.	18	18
Having lots of reading for homework.	15	9
Having a lively imagination.	13	15
Having lots of written exercises.	8	6
Being told how to do it.	8	9

Inspection of this table reveals a similar pattern of popularity for both age groups. Most students give priority to *liking it, having lots of time for reading*, and *concentrating well*. The older students give more weight to *learning the meaning of lots of words* and *having many good books available* than the younger ones did, and understandably less to *sounding out the words*, a skill hopefully learned at an earlier age. Few students see much virtue, in any country, in *written exercises*, in *reading homework*, or in *being told how to do it*. Most seem to support the view that one improves one's reading with regular, interesting, concentrated reading.

An examination of the patterns of responses for each country was not immediately fruitful, as the similarities were more apparent than the differences. It is possible that many of the less able 9-year-olds were unable to respond with adequate insight to produce meaningful results. Therefore an analysis was made of the best five percent of readers in each country, as judged by the students' average score across all domains. These students typically scored above 600 points except in two or three low-scoring countries.

The percentage of "best readers" at Population A level in each country was tabulated and converted into standard scores to reveal more readily any cross-cultural deviations. These scores were then plotted in Figure 8.1 for the ten highest-scoring and ten lowest-scoring countries, in order to identify patterns of response which were associated with more successful and less successful reading programs. This figure shows clear contrasts on strategies 4, 5, 6, 7, 9 and 10. (The values for Figure 8.1 can be found in Appendix G.)

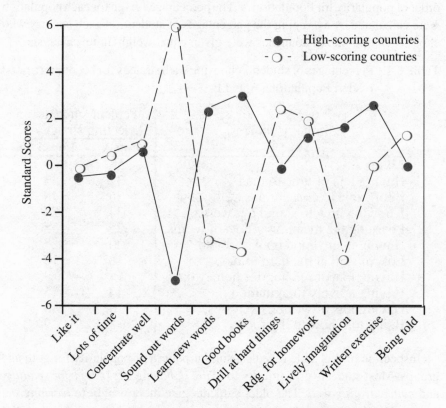

Figure 8.1. Ways to become a good reader: Responses from the top five percent of students in the ten highest-scoring and the ten lowest-scoring countries: Population A

Thus high-scoring countries differed from low-scoring countries in the following ways. Students who were good readers in the high-scoring countries more often believed that one becomes a good reader by:

1. Having many good books around
2. Having a lively imagination
3. Learning many new words
4. Doing many written exercises

They saw little value in being able to sound out the words, or having lots of drill at the hard things. By contrast, the best readers in the low-scoring countries claimed that good reading will result if one:

1. Learns how to sound out the words
2. Has regular drill at the hard things
3. Does much reading for homework

They see much less value in having a plentiful supply of good books, or having a lively imagination.

As the best readers in most of these countries were of similar ability, it is reasonable to conclude that these contrasting views of the good readers reflect different philosophies of reading instruction in these systems of education. While the two groups of students have learned to excel in reading by means of different approaches, the fact that one style has apparently prevailed in the countries with greater numbers of competent readers should not be overlooked. Further analysis of clusters in these responses is clearly warranted.

At Population B level, very similar trends emerged. Good readers in the highest-scoring countries valued a plentiful supply of good books, a lively imagination, liking it and having lots of time. Good readers in the lowest-scoring countries saw little point in many books or liking reading, but put relatively more emphasis on being able to sound out the words, drilling the hard things, and being able to concentrate. Once again, reading was apparently seen in these countries as a serious, difficult process, requiring hard work and disciplined effort. In the high achieving countries it was viewed more as a pleasant, imaginative activity.

CHAPTER NINE

VOLUNTARY READING PATTERNS

One goal of reading instruction which is given high priority in most countries is the development of voluntary reading habits in children. Teachers, principals and most parents would like students to read regularly as a voluntary activity, both in and out of school. Researchers have shown that time invested in reading raises achievement levels (Morrow and Weinstein 1986, Anderson et al. 1985) and helps citizens participate productively in their society (Graff 1981, Goody 1968).

However, the extent of students' reading activity is rarely assessed in any formal or systematic fashion. Certainly there have been numerous surveys of students' reading interests in many of the participating countries, and there is a limited body of evidence about the consistent factors that influence children's reading activity (Guthrie and Greaney 1991).

It is a matter of concern to educators that a number of studies indicate that reading activity out of school is declining in spite of the greater variety of attractive books and magazines available to today's young people. Surveys conducted in the UNITED STATES, IRELAND, ENGLAND, SCOTLAND, and NEW ZEALAND, among others, have drawn attention to the small numbers of books read by typical students in their own leisure time (Guthrie and Greaney 1991), while classroom observation studies have often shown that too little reading occurs in school. For many students, then, the research appears to show that reading is something separate from real life, something to be learned at school and then used only if it cannot be avoided. If reading has a key role to play in extending students' interests and knowledge and preparing them for the work-place, then a balanced reading program should give students both the ability to read and the desire to do so. Without this desire, students will not participate fully in their society.

An international survey provides an ideal opportunity to compare the voluntary reading activities reported by students of comparable ages in different countries.

How were students' voluntary reading activities assessed?

All students at each Population level were asked to complete a questionnaire which was intended to reveal how often and what sort of materials they read, at home and in school. The study of reading activity by means of questionnaires has a long established tradition in many of the participating countries, although the IEA researchers had no illusions about the problems of measurement involved. Within the limitations of time, national traditions and funding, it proved to be the only feasible approach.

Cross-cultural studies of reading interests have of course been attempted before using the same methodology. Thorndike (1973) surveyed the reading attitudes of 10- and 14-year-olds in 15 countries by means of questionnaire, and found consistently positive but low correlations between reported attitudes to reading and achievement in reading comprehension. In a parallel study of literature achievement, Purves (1973) found slightly higher correlations between interest in literature and students' achievement scores at both the 14-year-old and pre-university levels.

Greaney and Neuman (1990) used students' essays and questionnaires to analyze the functions of students' leisure reading at three age levels (8, 10 and 13) in 15 countries, and found clear similarities across ages and cultures in the reported purposes of children's reading. Persistent gender differences in reading interests across countries have been revealed in this and in other studies, in a variety of countries (e.g., Greaney [Ireland] 1980, Robinson and Weintraub [United States] 1973, Bardsley [New Zealand] 1991, Whitehead, Cappey, Maddren and Wellings [England] 1977). Girls are found to read more often than boys, to read more often for enjoyment, and to prefer reading about a wider range of topics than the boys do.

In a report for Unesco, Guthrie and Siefert (1984) summarized a set of surveys of reading activity in several countries, using a variety of methods.

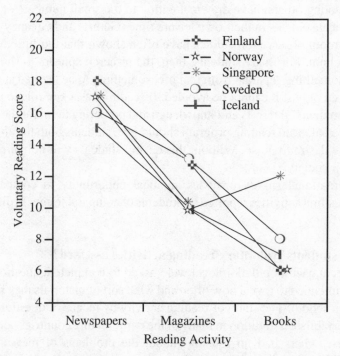

Figure 9.1. Voluntary reading: Countries with students favoring
newspapers: Population B

Prominent among them was an interview study conducted in 12 countries (Szalai 1972). Adult participants kept diaries of their use of time, and results showed many consistencies across cultures in the adults' leisure activities.

The actual questions used in the IEA survey were pilot tested and revised in most of the participating countries. These trials showed the benefits of having the test administrators read the questions aloud to the 9-year-old students, and allowing them ample time to complete them.

The major disadvantages of questionnaires in this context are widely known. When asked to estimate how often they read, students, especially at young age levels, often lack the insight to generalize about their behavior. Many literally do not know how many books they normally read in a week. Moreover, in many cultures students experience a strong pressure to respond according to what they believe the teachers, or other authorities would expect. This "compliance effect" or "social desirability factor" appears to vary across cultures, and probably distorts the univariate analysis reported here. Thus caution has been observed in the reporting, and is recommended in the interpretation. Where there are patterns of responses which indicate such desirability effects the results are not reported. The bulk of this section will focus on Population B results, which show evidence of higher reliability.

Patterns of Voluntary Reading Activity

Population B students were asked to estimate how often they read different kinds of books, magazines and newspapers, using a six point scale which varied from *Almost Never* to *Almost Every Day*. Students made ratings for 15 kinds of books, eight types of magazines and seven sections of newspapers. The scores for each scale were calculated to produce Total Voluntary Reading scores in each category – books, magazines and newspapers – for each student. These voluntary reading scores revealed different patterns of popular reading material in many countries.

Figure 9.1 presents the voluntary reading scores for the countries where newspapers were read with greater frequency than magazines or books. Newspapers are clearly very popular in most Scandinavian countries and SINGAPORE; by contrast books are seldom read by students in these countries with the exception of SINGAPORE. (The values for the figures in this chapter can be found in Appendix G.)

Figure 9.2 presents the corresponding profiles for those countries in which magazines were more widely read. The countries which reported reading books more frequently than magazines or newspapers were all developing countries. As magazines and newspapers are less plentiful in these countries, the relative popularity of books may reflect the fact that books are more accessible from school. Figure 9.3 shows the high book reading patterns of these countries.

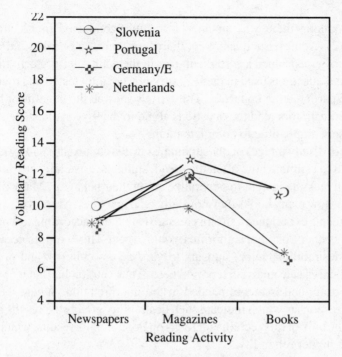

Figure 9.2. Voluntary reading: Countries with students favoring
magazines: Population B

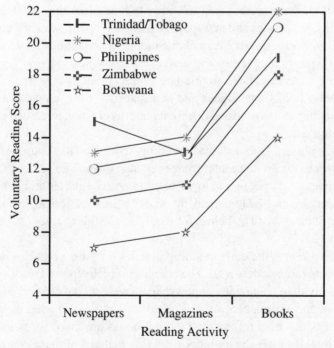

Figure 9.3. Voluntary reading: Countries with students
favoring books: Population B

Not all countries showed unbalanced profiles. For contrast, Figure 9.4 presents the results for those countries which showed uniformly high and uniformly low patterns of reading activity among 14-year-olds. All forms of reading are popular in GREECE and HUNGARY. The countries in the lower half of the figure show low levels of voluntary reading of all types.

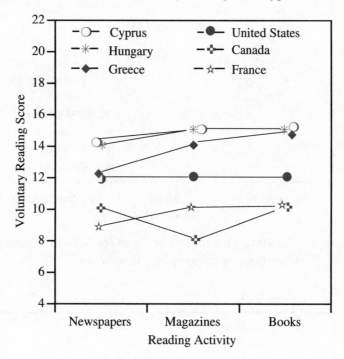

Figure 9.4. Voluntary reading: Countries with evenly distributed preferences: Population B

Voluntary reading and access to books

Not all students have ready access to reading materials. Likewise there are many students who are surrounded by books but who do not often read them.

To what extent is voluntary reading a function of the reading availability of books at home? To investigate this matter, the total voluntary reading score was related to selected categories taken from the *Books in the Home* scale as reported by the 14-year-old students. In seven countries there was a strong relationship revealed between the number of books reported in the students' homes and the total amount of their voluntary reading across books, magazines, and newspapers. Figure 9.5 shows that the relationship was strongest in TRINIDAD AND TOBAGO. Students in SINGAPORE who have fewer than ten books at home read very little (score = 32). Those who report over 200 books at home read a great deal (score = 46).

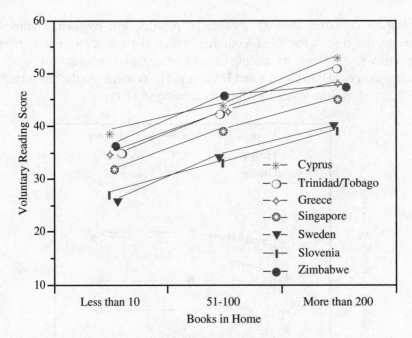

Figure 9.5. Voluntary reading by books in the home: Countries
with strong relationship: Population B

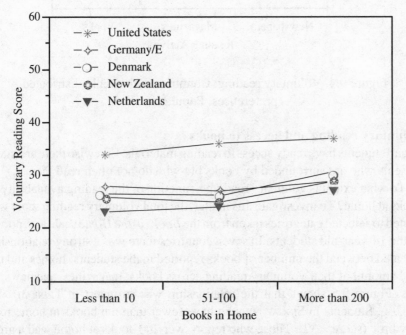

Figure 9.6. Voluntary reading by books in the home: Countries
with slight relationship: Population B

By contrast, there are five countries where the level of book ownership is largely unrelated to the amount of reading done (Figure 9.6). Several of these are countries with large school libraries and plentiful reading resources in the community. The students in these countries would therefore be less dependent on having a ready supply of books at home.

Amount of voluntary reading by achievement level

Numerous researchers have demonstrated that students who read often read well. There is a positive correlation between volume of reading and achievement levels. Is this generalization true for every country?

In the present survey, Population A students were asked to estimate on a four point scale how often they read books, magazines, comics and newspapers in their leisure time. Their estimates were totaled, and the sums classified by quartiles, that is, the 25 percent who read the least to the 25 percent who read the most. Then the total achievement means of students in each quarter were calculated.

Figure 9.7 shows the results of this analysis for Population A for the average of all countries and for seven individual countries. The general pattern is that students who read least in their spare time have the lowest average scores. In all 27 countries, there was also a steady trend upward in achievement to the third quarter of voluntary reading, and in ten systems, to the highest quarter. On the other hand there were fifteen countries where there was a peak at the third quarter and a slight descent to the highest quarter (Figure 9.8). While this link does not prove the old adage that "one learns to read by reading" it is certainly consistent with such advice. The best readers do read often in all countries.

At the Population B level the link between regular book reading and achievement declines (Figure 9.9). In BOTSWANA, ZIMBABWE, VENEZUELA, the PHILIPPINES, FINLAND, SWEDEN and SLOVENIA, frequent readers still read best, but in 24 countries the trend was different. The highest achievement was shown by those in the second or third quarters at this stage of their schooling. If there are direct benefits to be obtained from regular reading at this age, they appear to reach a peak at relatively low levels of voluntary reading in most systems. In the developing countries, however, it is clear from Figure 9.9 that most students do not reach that optimum level, even in the highest quarter of voluntary reading. The contrast between the trend lines in the top and bottom half of Figure 9.9 is quite striking.

Thus the benefits of frequent voluntary reading were most obvious at a younger age and, at the 14-year-old level in some of the countries. These findings are consistent with the principle that regular plentiful reading is important to attain a high level of reading ability, as measured by these tests, but is less crucial for sustaining it.

The patterns observed in magazine reading were similar to those of book reading, with a decrease in achievement in the highest levels of voluntary

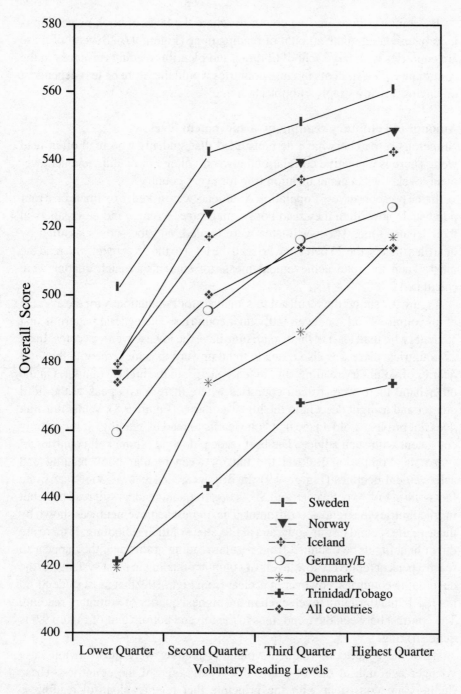

Figure 9.7. Population A: Reading achievement closely related to levels of
voluntary reading

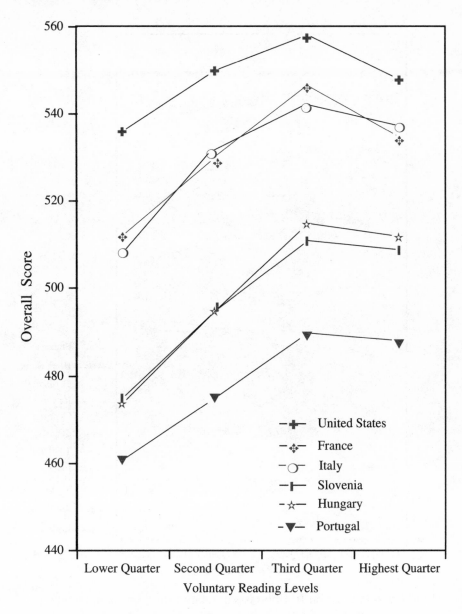

Figure 9.8. Population A: Reading achievement peaks in
third quarter of voluntary reading

reading. With newspaper reading the positive relationships with reading achievement were even more obvious. In 21 countries, the highest scoring students were
the most frequent newspaper readers.

Further detailed analyses of students' voluntary reading will be reported in
other publications.

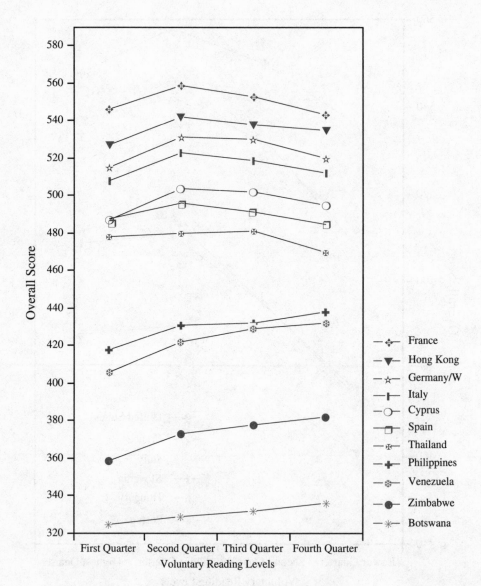

Figure 9.9. Population B: Contrasts in relationships between reading
achievement and voluntary reading levels

REFERENCES

Anderson, R. C., Hiebert, E. H., Scott, J. A. & Wilkinson, I. A. G. (1985). *Becoming a National of Readers: The Report of the Commission on Reading.* Washington, DC: National Institute of Education.

Anderson, L. W., Ryan, D. W., & Shapiro, B. J. (Eds.). (1989). *The IEA Classroom Environment Study. International Studies in Educational Achievement:* Vol. 4. Oxford: Pergamon Press.

Bardsley, D. (1991). Factors Relating to the Differential Reading Attitudes, Habits and Interests of Adolescents. New Zealand: Massey University.

Calfee, R. & Drum, P. (1986). Research on teaching reading. In M. C. Wittrock (Ed.), *Handbook of Research on Teaching* (3rd Edition) New York: Longman.

Downing, J. (1972). *Comparative Reading.* New York: MacMillan.

Elley, W. B. (1991) Acquiring literacy in a second language: The effect of book-based programs. *Language Learning, 41*(3), 375-411.

Elley, W. B. & Mangubhai, F. (1992). Multiple choice and open-ended items in reading tests. *Studies in Education Evaluation, 18*(2), 191-199.

Elley, W. B. & Tolley, C. W. (1972). *Children's Reading Interests.* Wellington, N. Z.: Council for Educational Research.

Fuller, B. (1987). What school factors raise achievement in the third world? *Review of Educational Research, 57*(3) 255-292.

Goody, J. (Ed.). (1968). *Literacy in Traditional Societies.* Cambridge: Cambridge University Press.

Graff, H. J. (Ed.). (1981). *Literacy and Social Development in the West:: A Reader.* Cambridge: Cambridge University Press.

Greaney, V. (1980). Factors related to the amount and type of leisure time reading. *Reading Research Quarterly, 15*(3) 337-57.

Greaney, V. & Neuman, S. B. (1990). The functions of reading. *Reading Research Quarterly, 25*(3) 172-195.

Guthrie, J. T. & Greaney, V. (1991). Literacy acts. In R. Barr, M. L. Kamil, P. Mosenthal, & P. D. Pearson (Eds.), *Handbook of Reading Research:* Vol. II. New York: Longman.

Guthrie, J. T. & Siefert, M. (1984). *Measuring Readership: Rationale and Technique*. Paris: Unesco.

Hiebert, E. H. & Calfee, R. C. 1992. Assessing literacy: From standardized tests to portfolios and performances. In S. J. Samuels and A. E. Farstrup (Eds.). *What Research Has to Say About Reading Instruction* (2nd ed.). Newark: IRA.

Johnson, D. D. (1974). Sex differences in reading across cultures. *Reading Research Quarterly*, *9*(1) 67-86.

Kyöstiö, O. K. (1980). Is learning to read easy in a language in which the grapheme-phoneme correspondences are regular? In J. F. Kavanagh & R. L. Venezky (Eds.), *Orthography, Reading and Dyslexia*. Baltimore: Baltimore University Press.

Lapointe, A. E., Mead, N. A. & Phillips, G. W. (1989). *A World of Differences: An International Assessment of Mathematics and Science*. Princeton, NJ: ETS.

Levine, K. (1986). *The Social Context of Literacy*. London: Routledge & Kegan Paul.

Lundberg, I. & Hoien, T. (Eds.). (1991). *Literacy in a World of Change: Perspectives on Reading and Reading Disability*. Stavanger: Center for Reading Research.

Malmquist, E. (1991). Literacy in the world: Myths and realities. In I. Lundberg & T. Hoien (Eds.), *Literacy in a World of Change: Perspectives on Reading and Reading Disability*. Stavanger: Center for Reading Research.

Morrow, L. & Weinstein, C. (1986). Encouraging vocabulary reading: The impact of the literature program on children's use of library centers. *Reading Research Quarterly*, *21*(3), 330-346.

Neuman, S. B. & Koskinen, P. (1992). Captioned television as comprehensible input. *Reading Research Quarterly*, *27*(1) 94-106.

Oney, B. & Goldman, S. R. (1984). Decoding and comprehension skills in Turkish and English: Effects of the regularity of grapheme-phoneme correspondences. *Journal of Educational Psychology*, *76*(4) 557-568.

Postlethwaite, T. N. & Wiley, D. E. (1992). *The IEA Study of Science II: Science Achievement in 23 Countries*. Oxford: Pergamon Press.

Preston, R. C. (1962). Reading achievement of German and American children. *School and Society*, *90*, 350-354.

Purves, A. C. (1973). *Literature Achievement in 10 Countries*. Stockholm: Almqvist & Wiksell.

Robinson, H. M. & Weintraub, S. (1973). Research related to children's interests and development values of reading. *Library Trends, 22*, 81-108.

Shin-Ying Lee, Stigler, J. W. & Stevenson, H. W. (1988). Beginning reading in Chinese and English. In B. R. Foorman & A. W. Siegel (Eds.), *Acquisition of Reading Skills: Cultural Constraints and Cognitive Universals*. Hillsdale: University of Houston.

Stanovich, K. E. (1991). Word recognition: Changing perspectives. In R. Barr, M. L. Kamil, P. Mosenthal & P. D. Pearson (Eds.), *Handbook of Reading Research:* Vol. II. London: Longman.

Steffenson, M. S., Joag-Dev, C. & Anderson, R. C. (1979). A Cross-cultural perspective on reading comprehension. *Reading Research Quarterly, 15*(1) 10-29.

Szalai, A. (Ed.). (1972). *The Use of Time: Daily Activities of Suburban and Urban Populations in 12 Countries*. The Hague: Mouton.

Thorndike, R. L. (1973). *Reading Comprehension Education in Fifteen Countries*. Uppsala: Almqvist & Wiksell.

Unesco. (1991). World Education Report 1991. Paris: Unesco.

Wagner, D. A. (1991). Literacy in a global perspective. In I. Lundberg & T. Hoien (Eds.), *Literacy in a World of Change: Perspectives on Reading and Reading Disability*. Stavanger: Center for Reading Research.

Whitehead, F., Capey, A., Maddren, W. & Wellings, A. (1977). *Children and Their Books*. London: MacMillan.

APPENDIX A

PERSONNEL OF
THE IEA READING LITERACY STUDY

International Coordinating Center Staff
University of Hamburg, Germany
T. Neville Postlethwaite, International Coordinator (1989-1991)
Andreas Schleicher, Data Manager (1989-1992); International Coordinator
    (1991-1992)
Dieter Kotte, Asst. International Coordinator (1989-1990)
R. Elaine Degenhart, Asst. International Coordinator (1990-1992)

International Steering Committee
Warwick B. Elley, University of Canterbury, New Zealand (Chair)
John T. Guthrie, University of Maryland, United States (1989-1991)
Ingvar Lundberg, University of Umea, Sweden
Francis Mangubhai, University of Southern Queensland, Australia
Alan C. Purves, State University of New York-Albany, United States
    (Standing Committee Representative)
Kenneth N. Ross, Deakin University, Australia (Sampling Referee)

Technical Advisors
Albert E. Beaton, Educational Testing Service, Princeton, NJ United States
Nadir Atash, Westat, Rockville, MD United States
Peter Allerup, Danish Institute for Educational Research, Copenhagen,
    Denmark

National Research Coordinators
Dominique La Fontaine, University de Liège, BELGIUM
Serara Moahi, Ministry of Education, Gabarone, BOTSWANA
Victor Froese, University of British Columbia, Vancouver, BC CANADA
Constantinos Papanastasiou, Pedagogical Institute, Nicosia, CYPRUS
Jan Mejding, Danish Institute for Educational Research, Copenhagen,
    DENMARK
Pirjo Linnakylä, University of Jyväskylä, FINLAND
Emilie Barrier, Centre International d'Études Pédagogiques, Sèvres, FRANCE
Rainer Lehmann, University of Hamburg, GERMANY
Georgia Kontogiannopoulou-Polydorides, University of Patras, GREECE
Cheung Yat-shing, Hong Kong Polytechnic, HONG KONG
Judit Kádár-Fülöp, National Institute of Public Education, Budapest,
    HUNGARY

Sigridur Valgeirsdottir, Institute of Educational Research, Reykjavik, ICELAND

Jiyono, Balitbang Dikbud, Jakarta, INDONESIA

Michael O. Martin, St. Patrick's College, Dublin 9, IRELAND

Pietro Lucisano, Instituto di Filosofia (Pedagogia), Roma, ITALY

Kees de Glopper, S.C.O., Amsterdam, NETHERLANDS

Hans Wagemaker, Ministry of Education, Wellington, NEW ZEALAND

Samuel O. Ayodele, University of Ibadan, NIGERIA

Finn Egil Tønnessen, Senter for Leseforsking, Stavanger, NORWAY

Mona D. Valisno, National Educational Testing and Research Center, Manila, PHILIPPINES

Maria José Rau, Ministério de Educacào, Lisbon, PORTUGAL

Beatrice Tay, Ministry of Education, SINGAPORE

Marjan Setinc, University of Ljubljana, SLOVENIA

Guillermo Gil, Ministerio de Educación y Ciencia, Madrid, SPAIN

Karin Taube, University of Stockholm, SWEDEN

Francois Stoll, Psychologisches Institut, Zürich, SWITZERLAND

Malee Nitsaisook, Suan Sunandha Teachers' College, Bangkok, THAILAND

Hyacinth E. McDowall, Ministry of Education, Port-of-Spain, TRINIDAD AND TOBAGO

Marilyn Binkley, U.S. Department of Education, Washington D.C., UNITED STATES

Armando Morles, Universidad Pedagógica Experimental Libertador, Caracas, VENEZUELA

Rosemary Moyana, University of Zimbabwe, Harare, ZIMBABWE

APPENDIX B

INTERNATIONAL VALIDITY OF THE IEA READING LITERACY TESTS

How Comparable Across Countries Are the IEA Reading Literacy Tests?

There are many who would doubt the feasibility of developing a single test of reading literacy which is equally appropriate in all the languages and cultures represented in this study. This skepticism arises from a belief that literacy is so firmly entrenched in the culture, that what, and how, and how well a student typically reads is unique to each culture, and different from all others.

There are certainly many examples of reading exercises which have demonstrated such disparities. For instance, the ability of American students to read and comprehend a description of an Indian wedding, is clearly different from and inferior to that of Indian students reading the same description. Similarly in reading about a western wedding, Indian students have difficulties that American students avoid (see Steffenson et al. 1979). Each cultural group brings a different set of assumptions and different kinds of background knowledge which assist them in making the inferences necessary in any reading task. Such examples are common in our experience, and in the reading literature.

However, these graphic examples are carefully selected to make the point of cultural diversity. There exists also a set of reading materials which are common to all cultures and school systems, which are assumed to be known and understood by all. All countries have schools, with teachers, books, maps, graphs, timetables, and charts. All expect students to read and interpret fiction, to understand expository passages on familiar and unfamiliar topics, to study a range of similar topics in school and at home. Moreover, an earlier IEA study on classroom climate showed a remarkable similarity in school teaching and management patterns (Anderson et al. 1989). More generally, it should be noted that students are typically brought up in families by adults, with whom they have relationships which are sometimes in conflict. They nearly all have access to television, libraries, stores, newspapers, magazines and comics, and many of these variables are very similar across nations. Despite the obvious diversity, there is much common experience in the countries represented in this survey.

In planning the IEA reading literacy tests, it was the *common* features which were stressed. Passages dealing with topics unique to one culture were deliberately avoided.

Thus, the following measures were undertaken to enhance the comparability of the tests used in this project.

1. Discussions were held with National Research Coordinators (NRCs) to identify suitable and unsuitable topics for an international test.

2. Each country was asked to submit passages and items and 20 NRCs responded.

3. The passages were selected by an international committee and duly edited by NRCs and their National Advisory Committees.

4. All NRCs rated, for suitability, the passages and items proposed for the pilot tests, and unsuitable passages were dropped.

5. Passages and items were translated according to carefully laid-down guidelines, and checked for problems.

6. Cultural adaptations were made to the passages and items to ensure that peoples' names, place names, currencies and metrics were appropriate for each culture.

7. All countries participated in the pilot tests to help identify remaining items unsuitable for any culture. This was achieved by conducting item analyses on the results and studying the patterns of student responses across countries. Any items which behaved differently across nations according to these analyses were dropped or modified.

8. More specifically, Rasch analyses were undertaken on the results of both the pilot tests and the final tests, and any poor-fitting items were dropped. On the basis of this analysis, more than half the items were deleted after the pilot test at each age level. After the final test, six items were dropped from the Population A tests, and seven from the Population B tests. As the remaining test items were considered to be fitting the Rasch model well, within their respective domains, they were assumed to be measuring the same qualities in each country. In other words, the probability of a student getting any particular item correct, for a given level of score is the same for all countries.

9. As a further check, items were also examined by a correlational method, to ensure that they were behaving similarly in the final tests. Correlations were computed between the p values of the items in each domain in each country and the mean p values across all countries. These coefficients showed very high correlations between the difficulty indices across countries. That is, if an item was difficult in one country it was found to be difficult in all countries. When compared in this way the mean rank orders of item difficulties was approximately 0.92 for Population A and 0.91 for Population B.

10. Any single item which was poorly fitting in one country but not others was omitted from that country's results and the Rasch procedure used to estimate the students' scores fairly without it.

All these measures were taken to make the tests as appropriate as possible for each cultural group. Such measures are rarely undertaken so carefully within most countries. While some minor features may still be found to exist which a few observers would perceive as lending a cultural bias, the statistics reveal that students in each country did in fact respond in a similar fashion to the items, allowing for differences in ability. Moreover the items did behave in similar fashion in each country. In other words, the test results are believed to be comparable across countries, as they would be within countries.

Of course, it could be argued that by making the tests appropriate for all that they finished by being appropriate for no single country. Deletion of topics unique to any one culture could mean a test so devoid of interest that it lacks validity in all cultures.

A study of the test passages, however, shows that the range of topics is still very wide, wider indeed than that found in most single sets of standardized reading tests. In the light of these considerations, the reader can have reasonable confidence that the test results were as comparable across countries as is any standardized test within a single country. They are not perfect, but they provide a defensible basis for making comparisons in the three domains tested.

APPENDIX C
RATIONALE FOR SCORES USED

In studies of this kind, it sometimes is necessary to exclude one or more items from analysis after testing for reasons not anticipated prior to testing. It may be necessary, for example, to remove an item from analyses in all countries if it did not function in practice as intended. Or, if test completion rates are uniformly low across many countries, a decision may be made to not analyze responses to the last few items on a test.

Occasionally, an item is problematic in a particular country, perhaps because of errors of translation or some unanticipated country-specific consideration. When test results are analyzed using item response theory (IRT), it is possible to exclude items from analysis in particular countries without compromising the comparability of achievement measures across countries.

The purpose of removing items from analysis (either entirely or in particular countries) is to ensure that results reflect as accurately as possible student achievement levels in each country. In particular, the purpose is to ensure that students' results on individual items are providing information about the achievement domain being measured, and are not contaminated by differences in how tests have been translated or administered in different countries.

In this study, the question of excluding items from analysis arose as a result of known differences in testing conditions (e.g., times allowed for test completion) in different countries and because of an unusual level of non-completion of the test in some countries. Given the high non-completion rates, consideration was given to the possibility of basing each student's measure in the three reading domains on only the items obviously attempted by that student, excluding unanswered items at the end of the test. In this way, the influence of different testing conditions in different countries on students' reading scores might be reduced or eliminated.

Although a case for basing achievement measures on only obviously attempted items can be made, and may be appropriate in other IEA studies, this was not done in the current study for the following reasons:

1. The instructions to students were clear, that they should answer every item, that they should work quickly, and that they had 40 minutes to complete the test. Those students who followed these instructions and completed all items may well have been disadvantaged when their scores were compared with those who devoted all their time to the early part of the test, or were able to confine themselves to items they were sure about.

2. The time limits were agreed to by all NRCs and the Steering Committee during the test construction phase and were believed to be realistic. Students were allowed more than one minute per item.

3. In some countries where many items were "Not Reached" it was observed that students frequently omitted items early in the test. Thus, it is not clear which items were omitted and which were "Not Reached".

4. It is reasonable to suppose that many students failed to finish the tests because the longer and more difficult passages tended to be concentrated towards the end of the test sessions.

It is recognized that the style of response to formal tests may differ from one country to another. Thus, it is possible that scores may have been higher in countries which had many students who did not complete the test. Their traditions may have encouraged them not to respond when they were unsure. For these countries, the scores in this booklet may be an underestimate. Under the circumstances there is no ready way of estimating their scores precisely.

APPENDIX D

TARGET POPULATIONS AND SAMPLES

The two target populations were defined as follows:

Population A: All students attending mainstream schools on a full-time basis at the grade level in which most students were aged 9:00 - 9:11 years during the first week of the eighth month of the school year.

Population B: All students attending school on a full-time basis at the grade level in which most students are aged 14:00 - 14:11 years during the first week of the eighth month of the school year.

From the definitions it can be seen that students in separate special education schools were excluded from the defined populations.

Tables D.1 and D.2 present for Populations A and B the percentage of students omitted from the defined population, the percentage of students not given the tests in the classroom during the test administration, the number of schools or classes in the planned sample and the number of schools or classes in the achieved sample (i.e., the number of school or classes for which data are available in the data files handed in). Those not given the tests during the testing session were those deemed a) unable to take any items on the test because of learning or physical disability (typically mainstreamed children); or b) to have insufficient knowledge of the language of the test even to follow the general instructions (typically recent immigrants).

One prior requirement of the IEA Reading Literacy Study was that there should be a response rate of at least 80 percent of the schools or classes planned to be drawn. It will be noted that asterisks have been placed next to Nigeria, Thailand and Zimbabwe, countries which participated in Population B only. This is because the response rates were lower than 80 percent. Care should be exercised with data from these three populations.

Information is given below on the nature of the students omitted from the defined population or on the definition of the population. For example, in the first row of Tables D.1 and D.2 it can be seen that 3.6 percent and 3.8 percent of Belgian students have been omitted from Populations A and B respectively. In the notes below, it will be seen that these are students from schools in the francophone administered part of Belgium who were instructed in Flemish or German.

Table D.1. Information on omitted population, size of sample and school
           response rates for Population A

Country	POPULATION A					
	Students			Schools		
	% Excluded from defined pop.	% Excluded during test	Number in final sample	Planned	Achieved	% Response
Belgium.(Fr)	3.6	0.32	2729	150	149	99.3
Canada (BC)	1.2	2.33	2682	157	157	100.0
Cyprus	0.0	0.44	1515	182	181	99.5
Denmark†	0.0	3.27	3368	212	209	99.0
Finland	9.2	0.00	1557	71	71	100.0
France (State only)	16.0	0.00	1887	140	136	97.1
Germany (E)	0.0	0.13	1906	100	100	100.0
Germany (W)	0.0	0.85	2953	150	150	100.0
Greece	0.0	2.98	3616	176	175	99.4
Hong Kong	2.6	0.00	3312	167	167	100.0
Hungary	2.4	0.00	3174	144	144	100.0
Iceland (all schools)	0.5	1.43	4129	180	180	100.0
Indonesia (7 provinces only)	0.0	0.00	3393	176	174	98.9
Ireland	4.2	0.14	2783	134	122	91.0
Italy (state only)	8.6	1.10	2281	177	154	87.0
Netherlands	0.0	0.18	1737	91	91	100.0
New Zealand	0.0	0.32	3058	177	176	99.4
Norway	0.3	1.43	2566	191	191	100.0
Portugal (mainland only)	0.0	0.11	2799	165	145	87.9
Singapore (all schools)	0.0	0.68	7488	206	206	100.0
Slovenia	0.0	0.10	3421	140	140	100.0
Spain	11.1	0.00	8674	324	324	100.0
Sweden	0.0	0.91	4358	124	123	99.0
Switzerland	0.0	0.80	3411	225	225	100.0
Trinidad/Tobago†	0.0	0.01	3687	184	182	98.9
United States	4.9	2.33	6848	200	165	82.5
Venezuela	0.2	0.22	4819	181	161	89.0

†These systems sampled classes and not schools.

Table D.2.   Information on omitted population, size of sample and school
             response rates for Population B.

Country	POPULATION B					
	Students			Schools		
	% Excluded from defined pop.	% Excluded during test	Number in final sample	Planned	Achieved	% Response
Belgium.(Fr)	3.8	0.00	2796	153	144	91.7
Botswana	0.0	0.00	4768	137	137	100.0
Canada (BC)	1.1	0.38	4830	216	197	91.2
Cyprus (all schools)	0.0	0.07	1459	52	52	100.0
Denmark†	0.0	0.51	3832	207	209	100.0
Finland	12.4	0.00	1352	71	71	100.0
France (State only)	21.0	0.00	2582	140	136	97.1
Germany (E)†	0.0	0.12	1885	100	100	100.0
Germany (W)†	0.0	0.36	4302	200	196	98.0
Greece	1.4	0.39	3968	148	147	99.3
Hong Kong	1.2	0.00	3160	158	158	100.0
Hungary	0.25	0.00	3455	144	144	100.0
Iceland (all schools)	2.6	0.10	4000	124	124	100.0
Ireland	0.0	0.11	3817	162	151	93.2
Italy (state only)	4.8	0.80	3180	175	173	98.9
Netherlands	0.0	0.00	3897	174	162	93.1
New Zealand	0.0	0.34	3174	125	124	99.2
Nigeria*	0.0	0.00	2365	136	80	58.8
Norway	0.2	0.47	2446	142	138	97.2
Philippines	0.0	0.00	9713	245	244	99.6
Portugal (mainland only)	0.0	0.00	3529	136	130	95.6
Singapore (all schools)	0.0	0.00	4893	142	142	100.0
Slovenia	0.0	0.00	3328	139	139	100.0
Spain	6.5	0.00	8945	318	318	100.0
Sweden	0.0	0.52	3618	149	149	100.0
Switzerland	0.0	0.34	6488	362	322	89.0
Thailand*	0.8	0.00	2753	217	139	64.0
Trinidad/Tobago	0.0	0.00	3044	93	93	100.0
United States	4.9	0.58	3587	204	165	80.9
Venezuela	1.2	0.20	4434	178	162	91.0
Zimbabwe*	0.0	0.00	2749	192	143	74.5

†These systems sampled classes and not schools.
*These systems had a response rate of less than 80 percent.

Notes on Excluded Students
From Defined Target Populations

Belgium/French: All students in French-speaking Belgium instructed in Flemish or German were excluded.

Canada/BC: Students in Government Native Indian schools excluded.

Finland: Swedish speaking, special education, and laboratory schools excluded.

France: Overseas territories and private schools in mainland France were excluded. Private schools = 16 percent of all students at Pop A, 21 percent of all students at Pop B.

Germany/East: Students in special schools for the handicapped and institutions for specially talented students were excluded (8 percent).

Germany/West: Students in special schools for the handicapped and non-graded private schools were excluded (8.3 percent).

Greece: Pop B 1.4 percent in evening schools excluded.

Hong Kong: International schools, ESF Foundation schools, schools not participating in Secondary School Places Allocation System (SSPA) and schools with class size of less than 20 were excluded.

Hungary: Very small schools in remote areas and ungraded schools were excluded.

Iceland: Schools where there were fewer than 5 students in target population were excluded.

Indonesia: Excluded schools outside of Java, Riau (Sumatra) and East Nusa Tenggara. The included population accounts for 70 percent of the population.

Ireland: Private schools and schools with fewer than 5 students in the target population were excluded.

Italy: Non-government schools excluded.

Nigeria: Excluded schools outside of Lagos, Ogun, Oyo, Ondo, Bendel, Kwara.

Norway: Schools for Lapps excluded.

Philippines: Schools in earthquake and insurgency areas (about 39 percent of the population) excluded.

Spain: Students from schools with fewer than 10 students in the defined grade and from schools where medium of instruction not Castillian Spanish were excluded.

Thailand: Laboratory schools and schools controlled by the Department of Fine Arts and Culture.

United States: Fifty states (Mainland, Alaska and Hawaii) constituted the target population. Students in eligible schools not capable of taking test (about 4.9 percent of each population) were excluded.

Venezuela: Students attending private rural schools were excluded.

Standard Errors of Sampling

The standard errors of sampling were calculated by the jackknife technique. These are presented in various figures and tables.

Confidence Limits

Simultaneous confidence intervals controlling for all possible comparisons based on the Bonferroni procedures were calculated for the national mean scores presented in Figures 3.1, 3.2, 3.3 and 4.1, 4.2, 4.3 in the text.

APPENDIX E

ADJUSTMENT FOR AGE DIFFERENCES

It is clear from Tables 3.1 and 4.1 that the mean ages of the national samples of students varied somewhat from one country to another. Some variation was expected, as the target samples were selected by grade, not age. However, in Population A one country tested a sample whose mean age was 8.89 years, while four others had mean ages well above 10 years. At the Population B level, one sample had a mean age of 13.93 years, while seven others, mostly developing countries, had mean ages over 15.0 years.

To what extent would these departures from the defined samples affect the national means? Can these means be adjusted to compensate for these differences? There is no easy answer to these questions, as cross-sectional surveys do not normally provide enough information to make a reliable adjustment. However, the need for some such compensation was keenly felt by many in the project, so an approximation was attempted, using three independent approaches. Fortunately, all three converged on a similar outcome, so there are reasonable grounds for taking their results seriously.

1. Regression method

At each population level the correlation between the mean age of each country's sample and its mean composite score was calculated, and a regression equation used to estimate new mean scores with age equated. Those countries with much older students and relatively low scores were deliberately omitted from these calculations. The observed correlation between age and achievement was 0.21 (N = 25). The values for the slopes and intercepts were computed, the predicted scores were determined for each country and the residuals worked out. These were added to the country means, and the new values were taken as an approximate estimate of the country achievement means, on the assumption of equal age. The results of this exercise are shown in Tables E.1 (Population A) and E.2 (Population B). This analysis produced scores which were very close to the original means for most countries. The only large changes were in CANADA (BC) (+14), the NETHERLANDS (+9), PORTUGAL (-10), VENEZUELA (-15), and INDONESIA (-16). Thus a difference of 12 months produced a change of 18 to 20 points. At the 14-year-old level, the observed correlation between country mean age and mean composite score was again 0.21, and the resultant adjustments produced the following changes: CANADA (BC) (+18), ITALY (+16), HUNGARY (+14), SPAIN (+12), BELGIUM (FR) (+11), PORTUGAL (-20), FRANCE (-16), VENEZUELA (-18), ZIMBABWE (-17), and NIGERIA (-12). The remaining adjustments were relatively small.

Table E.1.   Mean scores in the booklet and scores adjusted for *age differences*
             for three domains for Population A.

	Narrative		Expository		Documents		
	Mean Scores	Adjusted for age	Mean Scores	Adjusted for age	Mean Scores	Adjusted for age	Score Difference
Belgium/Fr	510	509	505	504	506	505	-1
Canada/BC	502	516	499	513	500	514	+14
Cyprus	492	492	475	475	476	476	0
Denmark	463	463	467	467	496	496	0
Finland	568	569	569	570	569	570	+1
France	532	527	533	528	527	522	-5
Germany/E	482	487	493	498	522	527	+5
Germany/W	491	496	497	502	520	525	+5
Greece	514	521	511	518	488	495	+7
Hong Kong	494	491	503	500	554	551	-3
Hungary	496	503	493	500	509	516	+7
Iceland	518	518	517	517	519	519	0
Indonesia	402	386	411	395	369	353	-16
Ireland	518	525	514	521	495	502	+7
Italy	533	532	538	537	517	516	-1
Netherlands	494	503	480	489	481	490	+9
New Zealand	534	530	531	527	521	517	-4
Norway	525	525	528	528	519	519	0
Portugal	483	473	480	470	471	461	-10
Singapore	521	528	519	526	504	511	+7
Slovenia	502	503	489	490	503	504	+1
Spain	497	493	505	501	509	505	-4
Sweden	536	536	542	542	539	539	0
Switzerland	506	507	507	508	522	523	+1
Trinidad/ Tobago	455	458	458	461	440	443	+3
United States	553	549	538	534	550	546	-4
Venezuela	378	363	396	381	374	359	-15

Table E.2.   Mean scores in the booklet and scores adjusted for *age differences* for three domains for Population B.

	Narrative		Expository		Documents		
	Mean Scores	Adjusted for age	Mean Scores	Adjusted for age	Mean Scores	Adjusted for age	Score Difference
Belgium/Fr	484	495	477	488	483	494	+11
Botswana	340	341	339	340	312	313	+1
Canada/BC	526	544	516	534	522	540	+18
Cyprus	516	515	492	491	482	481	-1
Denmark	517	517	524	524	532	532	0
Finland	559	559	541	541	580	580	0
France	556	540	546	530	544	528	-16
Germany/E	512	515	523	526	543	546	+3
Germany/W	514	521	521	528	532	539	+7
Greece	526	534	508	516	493	501	+8
Hong Kong	509	498	540	529	557	546	-11
Hungary	530	544	536	550	542	556	+14
Iceland	550	548	548	546	509	507	-2
Ireland	510	516	505	511	518	524	+6
Italy	520	536	524	540	501	517	+16
Netherlands	506	515	503	512	533	542	+9
New Zealand	547	540	535	528	552	545	-7
Nigeria	402	390	406	394	394	382	-12
Norway	515	514	520	519	512	511	-1
Philippines	421	427	439	445	430	436	+6
Portugal	523	503	523	503	523	503	-20
Singapore	530	537	539	546	533	540	+7
Slovenia	534	534	525	526	537	538	+1
Spain	500	512	495	507	475	487	+12
Sweden	556	556	533	533	550	550	0
Switzerland	534	531	525	522	549	546	-3
Thailand	468	457	486	475	478	467	-11
Trinidad/ Tobago	482	489	485	492	472	479	+7
United States	539	532	539	532	528	521	-7
Venezuela	407	389	433	415	412	394	-18
Zimbabwe	367	350	374	357	373	356	-17

2. Growth from 9 to 14 years

The second approach taken was to estimate the amount of growth in all three domains, from 9 to 14 years, as indicated by gains on the common 14 anchor items, taken by students in both age groups, and then to divide by 5 to obtain an estimate of the amount of growth per year, on those items. This method produced the enclosed table of p values for each population, with the amount of growth calculated on the right.

Table E.3 shows that an overall gain of 23.7 points was demonstrated over five years on these common items. No doubt this figure would have been somewhat higher if there had not been a ceiling effect evident on some of the *Shark* items. On the admittedly debatable assumption of equal increments in achievement over each of the intervening five years, from 9 to 14 years, one would arrive at an estimate of growth of 4.74 percent per year, which is equivalent to 19 score points. If the two easiest *Shark* items were omitted from this calculation, the corresponding gains would be 5.15 percent, or 21 score points. These figures are very similar to those produced by the regression method (18 to 20 points per year).

Table E.3. Changes on anchor items from 9 to 14 years.

Passage	Item	Population A p value %	Population B p value %	Difference %
Temperature	1	73.1	86.7	13.6
	2	26.3	66.4	40.1
	3	38.8	69.1	30.3
	4	40.8	75.3	34.5
	5	63.6	89.8	26.2
Marmot	1	53.0	75.6	22.6
	2	49.0	81.0	32.0
	3	40.9	68.6	27.7
	4	40.0	71.6	31.6
Shark	1	78.4	89.8	11.4
	2	75.3	90.6	15.3
	3	74.6	86.5	11.9
	4	69.6	86.9	17.3
	5	68.0	85.6	17.6
Mean				23.7

3. Empirical comparison of adjacent age groups.

The empirical way to check the size of the gain in test scores over 12 months is to administer the tests to adjacent age groups from the same schools. Such a study was undertaken by the author in a small sample of five NEW ZEALAND schools with the Population A tests, administered under standardized conditions. The samples consisted of 212 students in Standards 3 and 4 (9- and 10-year-olds), in the same multigrade classrooms. As there is no difference in the curriculum or reading materials for these two grades, and as they were taught together in the same composite classes, the normal situation in NEW ZEALAND, it was assumed that variations in performance would be attributable to age, not to grade.

The results of this investigation showed that 10-year-olds performed slightly better than 9-year-olds on all items, and that an increase of 12 months of age was equivalent to a six percent gain in Total Score at the median (Table E.4). In schools where the 9-year-olds performed well there was an apparent ceiling effect which reduced these gains; in low scoring schools the gains were larger. While these figures might be found to vary slightly in other schools and other countries, they are reasonably consistent with the findings obtained by the other two methods. A gain of five to six percent per year, or approximately 20 points over 12 months is a reasonable estimate of growth. Hence the adjusted scores produced in Tables E.1 and E.2.

Table E.4.   Percentage mean scores on Population A tests (overall) for 9- and 10-year-olds by school

School	9-year-old mean	(N)	10-year-old mean	(N)	Growth (%)
A	73.5	35	78.1	31	4.6
B	67.0	31	70.5	32	3.5
C	62.0	9	70.0	12	8.0
D	51.4	11	59.6	15	8.2
E	50.0	21	62.9	15	12.9
Total	63.7	107	69.8	105	6.1

TABLE OF CORRELATIONS

Table F.1.   Intercorrelations for six basic indicators of national development (CDI), mean values, and total scores for Population A and Population B.

	1	2	3	4	5	6	7	8	Mean
1. GNP (Per capita in $ US)	1.00	.94	.69	-.73	.78	.63	.60	.64	10,076
2. Expenditure on education (per student in $ US)		1.00	.57	-.64	.76	.56	.46	.51	1,824
3. Life expectancy (in years)			1.00	-.93	.54	.85	.73	.73	72.5
4. % Low birth weight infants				1.00	-.66	-.78	-.69	-.69	7.6
5. Mean newspaper circulation (per 1000)					1.00	.57	.47	.61	236.4
6. % Adult literacy						1.00	.64	.70	91.9
7. Total score Pop A							1.00	.83	500.0
8. Total score Pop B								1.00	500.0

VALUES FOR FIGURES IN
CHAPTERS 6, 7, 8 AND 9

The values for each of the points plotted for the figures in Chapters 6, 7, 8 and 9 are given below. When available, the standard errors of sampling are also given

CHAPTER 6

Figure 6.2. Mean scores for seven countries with advantage for urban students, Population A

	Village	Small Town	Large Town	City
Greece	481	499	515	524
Hungary	481	509	515	519
Indonesia	383	425	431	450
Portugal	468	495	518	516
Slovenia	488	497	504	513
Trinidad/ Tobago	441	456	482	531
Venezuela	365	369	388	394

Figure 6.3. Mean scores for countries with negligible differences between urban and rural areas: Population A

	Village	Small Town	Large Town	City
Finland	568	568	572	571
United States	547	547	547	550
Sweden	540	546	529	535
Belgium/Fr	508	511	499	506
Denmark	470	468	482	481

Figure 6.4. Mean scores for three countries with advantage for rural students: Population A

	Village	Small Town	Large Town	City
New Zealand	542	533	526	525
France	537	531	519	523
Switzerland	515	513	507	504

CHAPTER 7

Figure 7.1. Average scores (with one standard error of sampling) by number of books in home: Selected countries compared with all countries: Population A.

	0	1-10	11-50	51-100	101-200	> 200
Finland	469 (59.2)	507 (17.0)	562 (7.8)	570 (5.8)	580 (6.7)	571 (6.1)
Hong Kong	484 (7.3)	514 (4.0)	532 (5.1)	533 (7.7)	527 (11.6)	519 (11.2)
Sweden	463 (46.7)	465 (22.2)	507 (10.5)	530 (7.4)	551 (6.4)	547 (4.4)
Trinidad/ Tobago	404 (17.1)	422 (8.5)	443 (6.1)	448 (6.8)	466 (8.4)	474 (5.5)
United States	484 (17.1)	506 (7.9)	525 (5.8)	553 (5.3)	570 (5.7)	555 (4.2)
Venezuela	357 (11.3)	379 (5.3)	389 (5.8)	398 (7.6)	394 (9.8)	400 (7.2)
All countries	430	458	487	501	514	513

Figure 7.2. Mean achievement by school library size: Population B

	Lowest quarter	2nd quarter	3rd quarter	Highest quarter
High CDI countries	521	525	536	535
All countries	492	500	504	515
Low CDI countries	445	452	454	474

Figure 7.6. Pattern of decreasing reading achievement with increasing TV viewing: Population A (with one standard error of sampling)

Hours viewing	Belgium/ French	France	Switzerland	United States	Germany/ West
0	522 (11.9)	536 (11.2)	535 (11.2)	564 (15.5)	495 (10.5)
0.5	508 (5.9)	540 (6.1)	514 (4.8)	554 (7.2)	515 (4.8)
1.5	517 (6.0)	537 (8.4)	515 (5.5)	561 (5.8)	508 (4.7)
2.5	512 (8.7)	533 (12.5)	508 (7.6)	558 (6.1)	499 (7.6)
3.5	497 (11.5)	524 (21.8)	494 (12.0)	551 (6.4)	493 (11.8)
4.5	493 (11.3)	497 (18.0)	482 (13.8)	544 (7.3)	478 (15.1)
5.5	483 (11.7)	476 (13.5)	477 (15.8)	527 (5.1)	472 (11.4)

Figure 7.7. Pattern of increasing reading achievement with moderately heavy
        TV viewing: Population A

Hours viewing	Finland		Italy		Norway		Portugal		Sweden	
0	550	(15.4)	515	(18.1)	528	(7.9)	438	(14.1)	517	(24.8)
0.5	569	(9.6)	536	(7.0)	522	(5.8)	468	(7.6)	532	(6.7)
1.5	572	(6.0)	532	(6.7)	529	(5.7)	475	(6.0)	545	(5.2)
2.5	572	(6.8)	534	(8.7)	532	(8.6)	488	(7.6)	546	(6.6)
3.5	578	(8.0)	543	(12.6)	536	(11.0)	492	(10.4)	551	(9.1)
4.5	559	(9.5)	516	(14.4)	519	(16.1)	491	(10.4)	536	(13.3)
5.5	555	(13.3)	503	(12.0)	508	(15.2)	478	(8.6)	493	(14.9)

(with one standard error of sampling)

CHAPTER 8

Figure 8.1. Ways to become a good reader: Responses from the top five percent
        of students in the ten highest-scoring and the ten lowest-scoring
        countries: Population A

	High-scoring countries	Low-scoring countries
Like it	-0.5	-0.2
Lots of time	-0.2	0.4
Concentrate well	0.6	0.7
Sound out words	-4.9	5.9
Learn new word	2.3	-3.2
Good books	3.0	-3.7
Drill at hard things	-0.3	2.4
Reading for homework	1.2	1.9
Lively imagination	1.7	-4.0
Written exercises	2.6	0.0
Being told	0.0	1.3

CHAPTER 9

Figure 9.1. Voluntary reading: Countries with students favoring newspapers: Population B

	News-papers	Magazines	Books
Finland	18	13	6
Norway	17	10	6
Singapore	17	10	12
Sweden	16	13	8
Iceland	15	10	7

Figure 9.2. Voluntary reading: Countries with students favoring magazines: Population B

	News-papers	Magazines	Books
Portugal	9	13	11
Germany/E	9	11	7
Netherlands	9	10	7
Slovenia	10	12	11

Figure 9.3. Voluntary reading: Countries with students favoring books: Population B

	News-papers	Magazines	Books
Trinidad/Tobago	15	13	19
Nigeria	13	14	22
Philippines	12	13	21
Zimbabwe	10	11	18
Botswana	7	8	14

Figure 9.4. Voluntary reading: Countries with evenly distributed preferences:
    Population B

	News-papers	Magazines	Books
Cyprus	14	15	15
Hungary	14	15	15
Greece	12	14	15
Canada/BC	10	8	10
United States	12	12	12
France	9	10	10

Figure 9.5. Voluntary reading by books in the home: Countries with strong
    relationship: Population B

	Less than 10	51-100	More than 200
Cyprus	39 (2.3)	44 (1.1)	53 (2.1)
Zimbabwe	36 (1.6)	45 (3.4)	48 (4.5)
Greece	35 (2.4)	43 (1.5)	49 (2.2)
Trinidad/Tobago	35 (4.8)	43 (1.1)	52 (0.7)
Singapore	32 (0.9)	39 (0.7)	46 (0.8)
Slovenia	28 (3.2)	33 (1.2)	39 (1.4)
Sweden	27 (2.9)	34 (1.1)	40 (0.9)

(with one standard error of sampling)

Figure 9.6. Voluntary reading by books in the home: Countries with slight
    relationship: Population B

	Less than 10	51-100	More than 200
United States	34 (4.9)	36 (2.6)	37 (2.1)
Germany/E	28 (3.2)	27 (1.2)	29 (1.2)
Denmark	27 (2.6)	26 (0.8)	30 (0.7)
New Zealand	27 (4.3)	25 (1.7)	29 1.3)
Netherlands	23 (3.5)	24 (1.6)	27 (1.3)

(with one standard error of sampling)

Figure 9.7. Population A: Reading achievement closely related to levels of voluntary reading.

	Lower quarter	2nd quarter	3rd quarter	Highest quarter
Sweden	502 (6.5)	542 (6.3)	551 (5.8)	561 (5.6)
Norway	476 (7.4)	524 (5.7)	538 (6.5)	547 (5.1)
Iceland	479 (0.0)	517 (0.0)	533 (0.0)	542 (0.0)
Germany/E	459 (8.4)	495 (8.5)	516 (8.6)	526 (7.9)
Denmark	419 (7.8)	474 (7.2)	489 (7.1)	517 (6.4)
Trinidad/Tobago	421 (5.6)	443 (5.4)	468 (6.0)	474 (6.1)

(with one standard error of sampling)

Figure 9.8. Population A: Reading achievement peaks in third quarter of voluntary reading.

	Lower quarter	2nd quarter	3rd quarter	Highest quarter
United States	536 (4.6)	550 (5.0)	558 (5.1)	548 (5.1)
France	512 (7.9)	530 (8.2)	546 (7,8)	536 (7.5)
Slovenia	475 (4.9)	495 (4.6)	511 (5.0)	509 (4.4)
Hungary	474 (5.4)	495 (5.2)	515 (5.0)	512 (5.0)
Portugal	461 (6.4)	475 (6.0)	490 (6.8)	488 (6.3)
Italy	508 (7.1)	531 (7.5)	542 (7.3)	538 (6.8)

(with one standard error of sampling)

Figure 9.9. Population B: Contrasts in relationships between reading achievement and voluntary reading.

	Lower quarter	2nd quarter	3rd quarter	Highest quarter
France	546 (6.5)	559 (6.4)	553 (6.4)	543 (6.4)
Hong Kong	527 (5.3)	542 (5.6)	538 (5.6)	535 (5.5)
Germany/W	515 (6.3)	531 (6.2)	530 (6.2)	520 (6.3)
Italy	508 (5.7)	523 (5.7)	519 (5.6)	512 (5.4)
Cyprus	485 (4.4)	504 (4.4)	502 (4.6)	495 (4.0)
Spain	488 (4.3)	496 (4.6)	491 (4.6)	485 (4.6)
Thailand	478 (9.1)	480 (8.9)	481 (8.7)	470 (9.2)
Philippines	418 (4.0)	431 (4.2)	432 (4.0)	438 (4.1)
Venezuela	406 (4.2)	422 (5.5)	429 (5.6)	432 (5.4)
Zimbabwe	359 (5.6)	373 (6.1)	378 (6.2)	382 (6.1)
Botswana	325 (4.0)	329 (4.2)	332 (4.3)	336 (4.2)

(with one standard error of sampling)

NOTES

NOTES

NOTES

NOTES

NOTES

NOTES

NOTES

NOTES

NOTES

NOTES